FAMILY PICTURES

Poems & Photographs Celebrating Our Loved Ones

To the families of the Virginia Tech students whose lives we remember and honor.

Published by Capital BookFest
Made possible by a generous contribution from Chick-fil-A Capital Centre
www.capitalbookfest.org

Photographs by Carol Siegel, from the Collection of the Alexandria Black History Museum, Alexandria, VA

ISBN: 978-1-888018-42-4

Art Direction: Sung Hee Kim/Sagetopia, LLC
Book Design: Rachel Ver Steeg/Sagetopia, LLC
Editorial Assistants: Dianne Beverly, Deanna Nikaido, Angela Boykin, and Carolyn Joyner.

10 9 8 7 6 5 4 3 2 1
Printed in the U.S.A.

FAMILY PICTURES

Poems & Photographs Celebrating Our Loved Ones

Edited by Kwame Alexander

With assistance by Dianne Beverly,
Deanna Nikaido, Angela Boykin,
and Carolyn Joyner

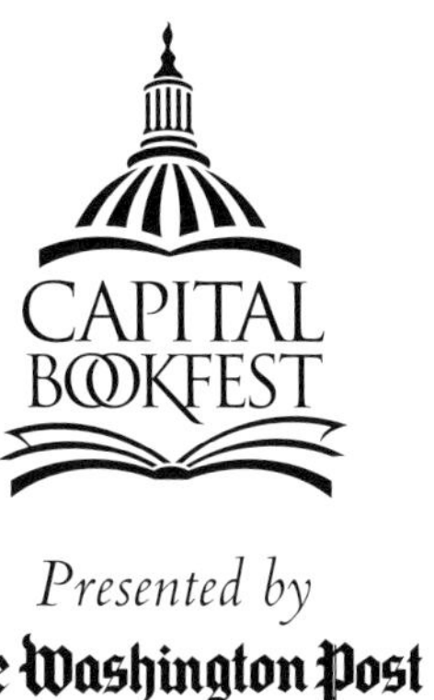

Presented by

The Washington Post

Table of Contents

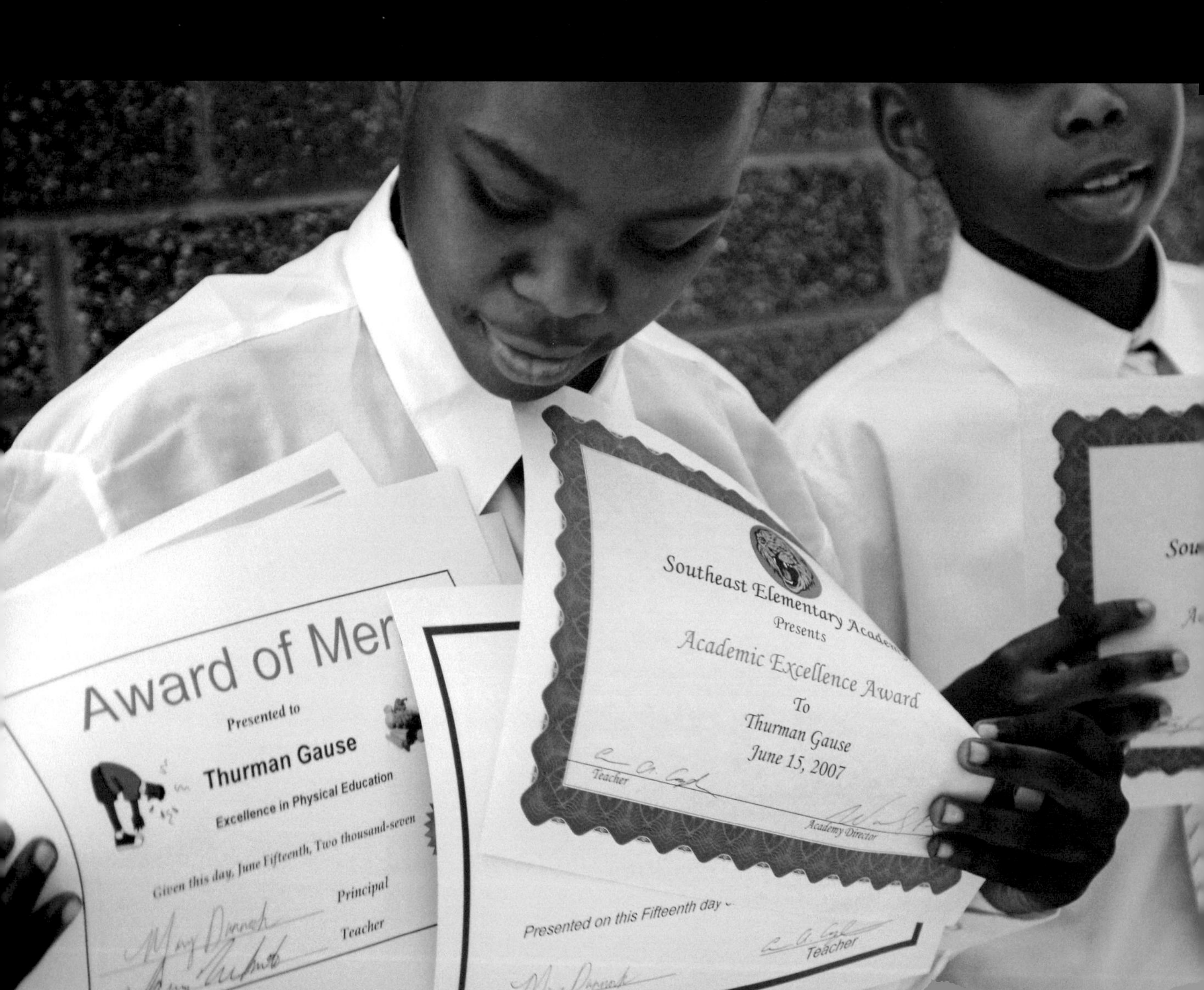
Award of Mer
Presented to
Thurman Gause
Excellence in Physical Education
Given this day, June Fifteenth, Two thousand-seven
Principal
Teacher
Southeast Elementary Acade
Presents
Academic Excellence Award
To
Thurman Gause
June 15, 2007
Teacher
Academy Director
Presented on this Fifteenth day
Teacher

Introduction

Here's what I remember: One hundred degree Sundays riding backseat in Dad's caramel Dodge Pinto, after church, sweat clinging like static; our heads out the window trying to catch a breeze. On our way to High's Ice Cream Store–Paradise. Meat Loaf. Summertime reunions with cousins unseen since last summer, barbecue for miles, aunts laughing at uncles dancing a lot, and drinking even more. Dominos and Bid Whist. The way the butter disappeared in Granny's rolls. The way I disappeared from Granny's switch. The stuff I found in Granddaddy's attic. Good Times. The time we sat, steel-like in fear, for two hours in an Orlando Hotel, Disney World a magnet to the three of us, because my father couldn't find his hat. The names I called my sisters. Bad. The looks they gave me. Worse. We found joy in traveling. Never minded moving. Living in New York, North Carolina, Virginia. In the same year. Counting cars, logging license plates, travel games. Winning the spelling bee. My father smiling. Relatives I never met. (And the ones I wish I hadn't). Loved ones who have passed. Uncle Richard. Granddaddy. Ovie. Granny. Aunt Dorothy. Granddaddy again. Funerals and meeting new folks and missing old ones. Family meetings. Which were more like lectures with no Q&A. Trials with no jury. The excitement around seven candles and seven days in December. My mother cooking. My father trying (Who ever heard of macaroni and cheese. And mustard?). Grocery store checkout line quizzes–*If I have a coupon for $.50 off and today is double coupon day and the Tropicana is on sale, 2 for $3, then what is the cost including tax*–with no reward for correct, and plenty of consequences for incorrect. Children playing, loving, smiling, planning, crying, dreaming, laughing, and leaping forever forward into their futures. I remember regularly sitting in the living room fingering through the countless memorabilia that my mother kept: scrapbooks, yearbooks, old report cards, portraits, love letters, wedding photos. I remember that in those Saturday morning sessions, I was looking for. . .me.

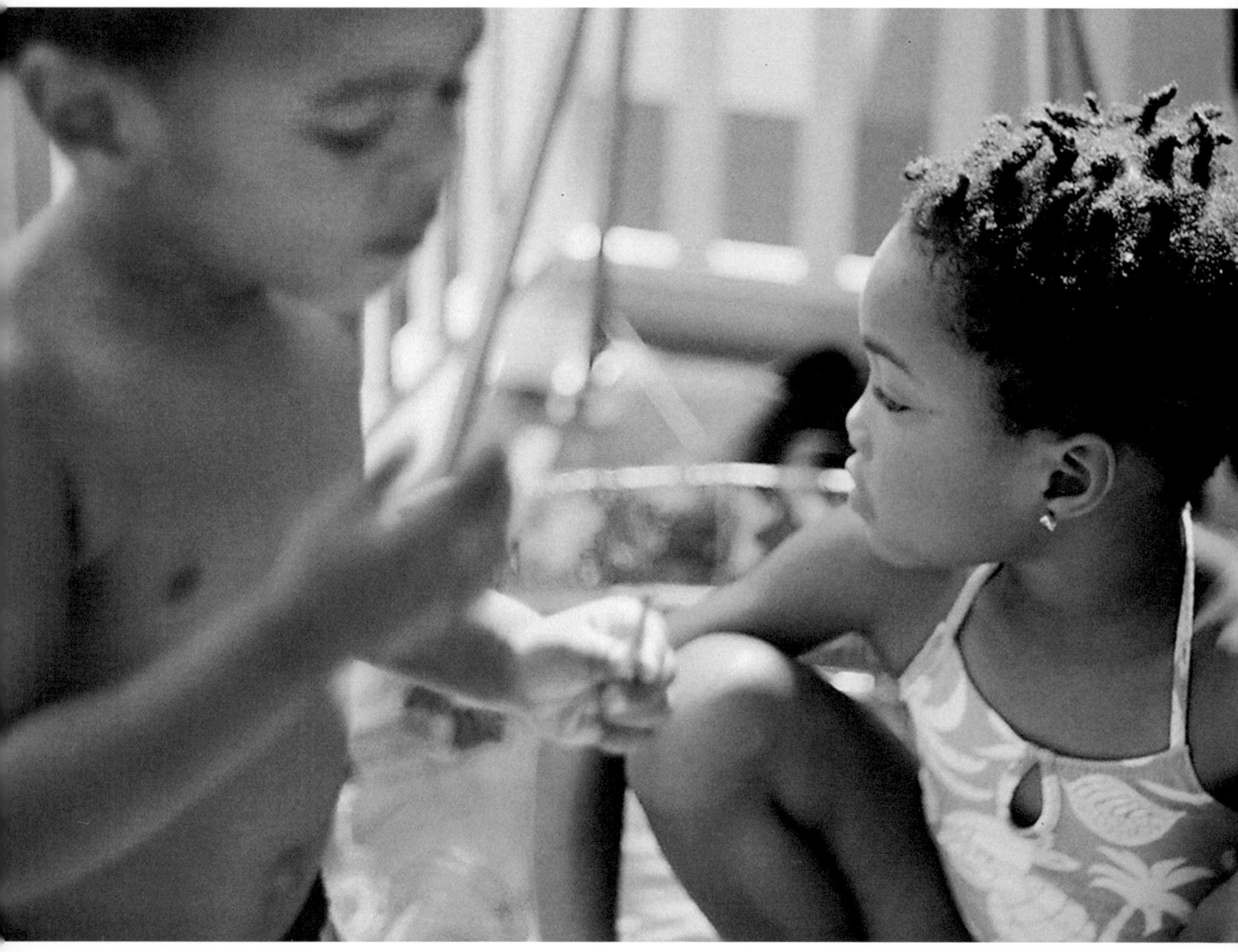

Here's what I know: I have my own family now, and we don't play spades, but we love scrabble. We've been to Jamaica and Disney World (No hats were lost). We've moved, on average, once every two years. My wife, from Louisiana, can burn in the kitchen, but I do most of the cooking (No mustard!). I wonder when did my mother find time to make meat loaf. When did Dad find time to play ping-pong with me? How did Granny make enough food for twenty hungry folks? Every Sunday. On my grandfather's salary alone. Am I a good father to my daughter? Do I talk too much to her? Was I this headstrong (cantankerous) as a teenager? As a child you never know the river of challenges your parents endure. As an adult, you wonder how you'll make it over without drowning, while your children swim–in Paradise.

This book is a celebration of the paradise of family. The woes and wonders In poetry and photographs, this book includes over 70 poets–new and established–and 10 photographers–award winning and emerging. Family Pictures aims to show the variety and value of family love, especially the joys of childhood. At the writing of this introduction, I am on a beach in North Carolina with my parents, siblings, niece, nephew, child, and wife. Inevitably someone will take a picture of a sister laughing; a brother frowning (after losing again at chess), children playing, and parents enjoying it all. Maybe I'll recite a couplet to calm everyone down at the dreaded family meeting. In these pages, the words and photographs are snapshots to remind us that no matter the time or circumstance–whether peril or promise–family matters and it always lasts. Good Times. Family Pictures is a cool ride we can all take and find... ourselves. Now, open your window, and enjoy our scrapbook.

Kwame Alexander
Cape Hatteras, NC
August 2007

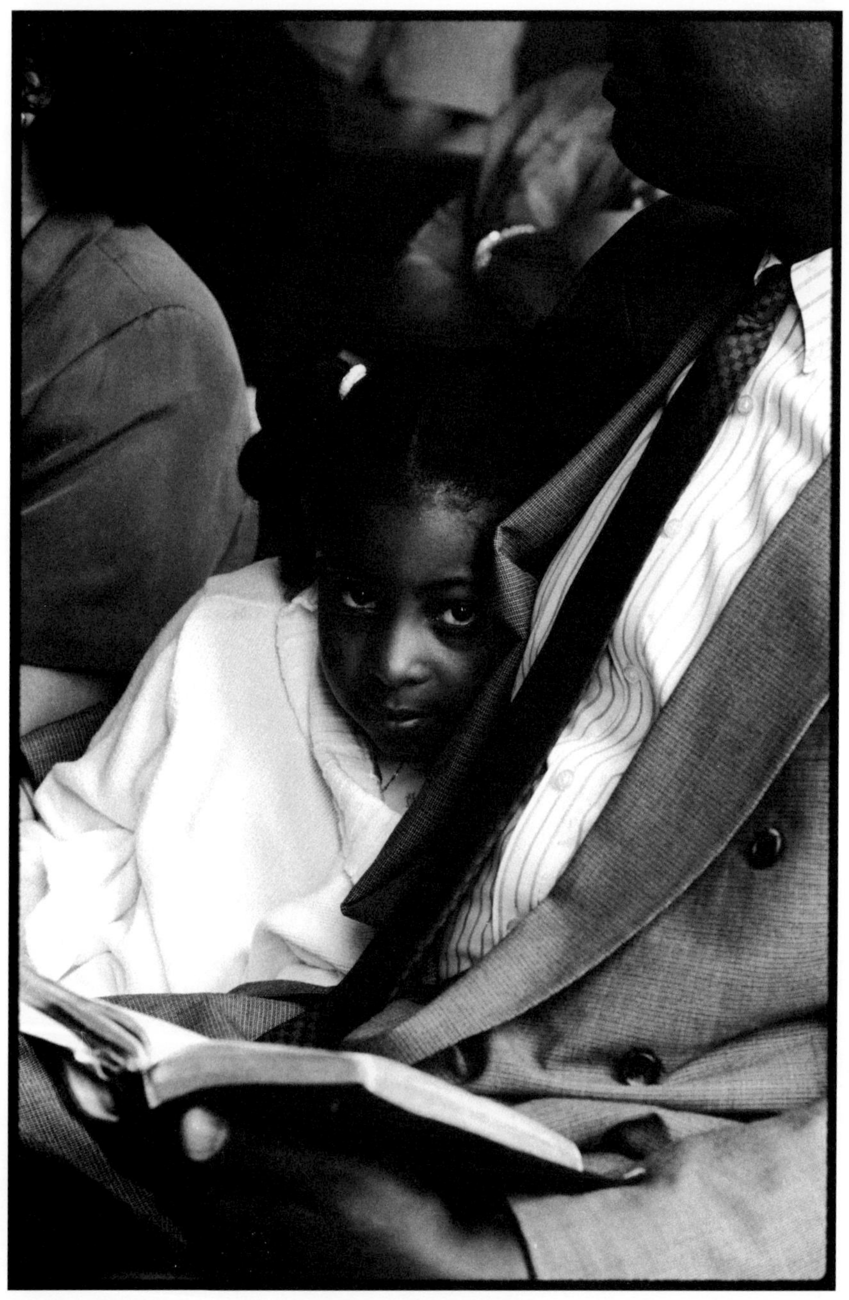

Breathing Lessons

Dedicated to Carl C. Wilson Sr.

At five, I remember
resting on Daddy's chest
nestled in his big arm chair
I rose and fell
into his heart's rhythm
I held the quiet
to learn the beats inside
kept up with its pace
by breathing deeper
held my air longer
to move with him
this safe space
cradled me in arms
strong as ancestral memory
gentle as the Caribbean Sea
here I found first love.

~ *Angela Boykin Turnbull*

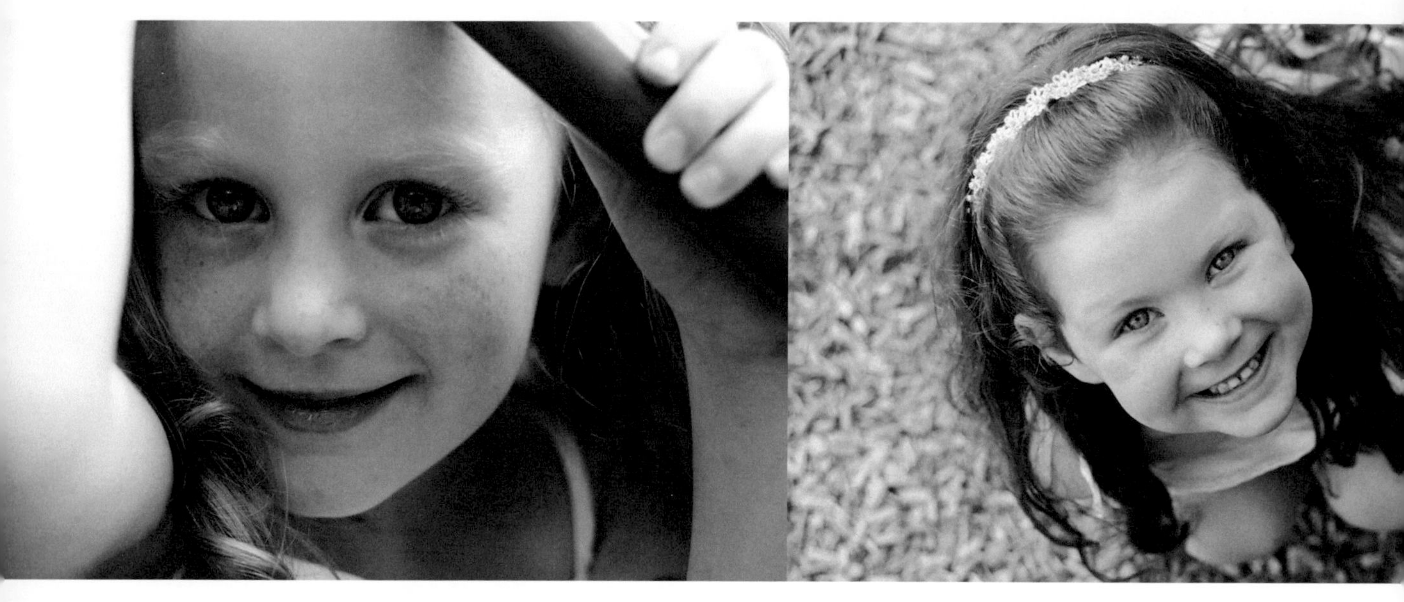

To Katharine: at Three

who runs past black bucket swings, sand,
bowls, and broken cups, past animals
that rock on heavy springs, who hoists herself
on the merry-go-round, waits for me,
who wobbles like a drunken sailor, who tilts
and whirls, wound-up clock without a key.
Carnival hypnotist, lazy pinwheel, master
of music-box pirouettes, you unfurl with the sun,
one hand over your head like in your first sleep.
You stamp your feet, fandango, and your arms
are cloud, your shoes are rain, you twirl
like a leaf, you dangle your castanets, you leap
off this spinning world, your arms are loaded
with stars, your arms are whorled with flowers.

~ *Joelle Biele*

Sitting with Daddy

you are finally home after seven sleeps
tired from the work
and the time away
bathed and wrapped in your burgundy robe
your hands are still black
your cheque still cash

I climb into your lap
your beard scratches
you are really there
I rest my head upon your chest
and listen to the thumpthump of your life

You read The Velveteen Rabbit to me
sounding one word at a time
deliberately following along
with your calloused finger:
when a child loves you   you become real

~ *Melissa Morelli Lacroix*

Ordinary Life

This was a day when nothing happened,
the children went off to school
remembering their books, lunches, gloves.
All morning, the baby and I built block stacks
in the squares of light on the floor.
And lunch blended into naptime,
I cleaned out kitchen cupboards,
one of those jobs that never gets done,
then sat in a circle of sunlight and drank
ginger tea, watched the birds at the feeder
jostle over lunch's little scraps.
A pheasant strutted from the hedgerow,
preened and flashed his jeweled head.
Now a chicken roasts in the pan,
and the children return, the murmur
of their stories dappling the air. I peel
carrots and potatoes without paring my thumb.
We listen together for your wheels on the drive.
Grace before bread. And at the table,
actual conversation, no bickering or pokes.
And then, the drift into homework.
The baby goes to his cars, drives them
along the sofa's ridges and hills.
Leaning by the counter, we steal a long slow kiss,
tasting of coffee and cream. The chicken's diminished
to skin & skeleton, the moon to a comma,
a sliver of white, but this has been a day of grace
in the dead of winter, the hard cold knuckle of the year,
a day that unwrapped itself like an unexpected gift,
and the stars turn on, order themselves into the winter night.

~ *Barbara Crooker*

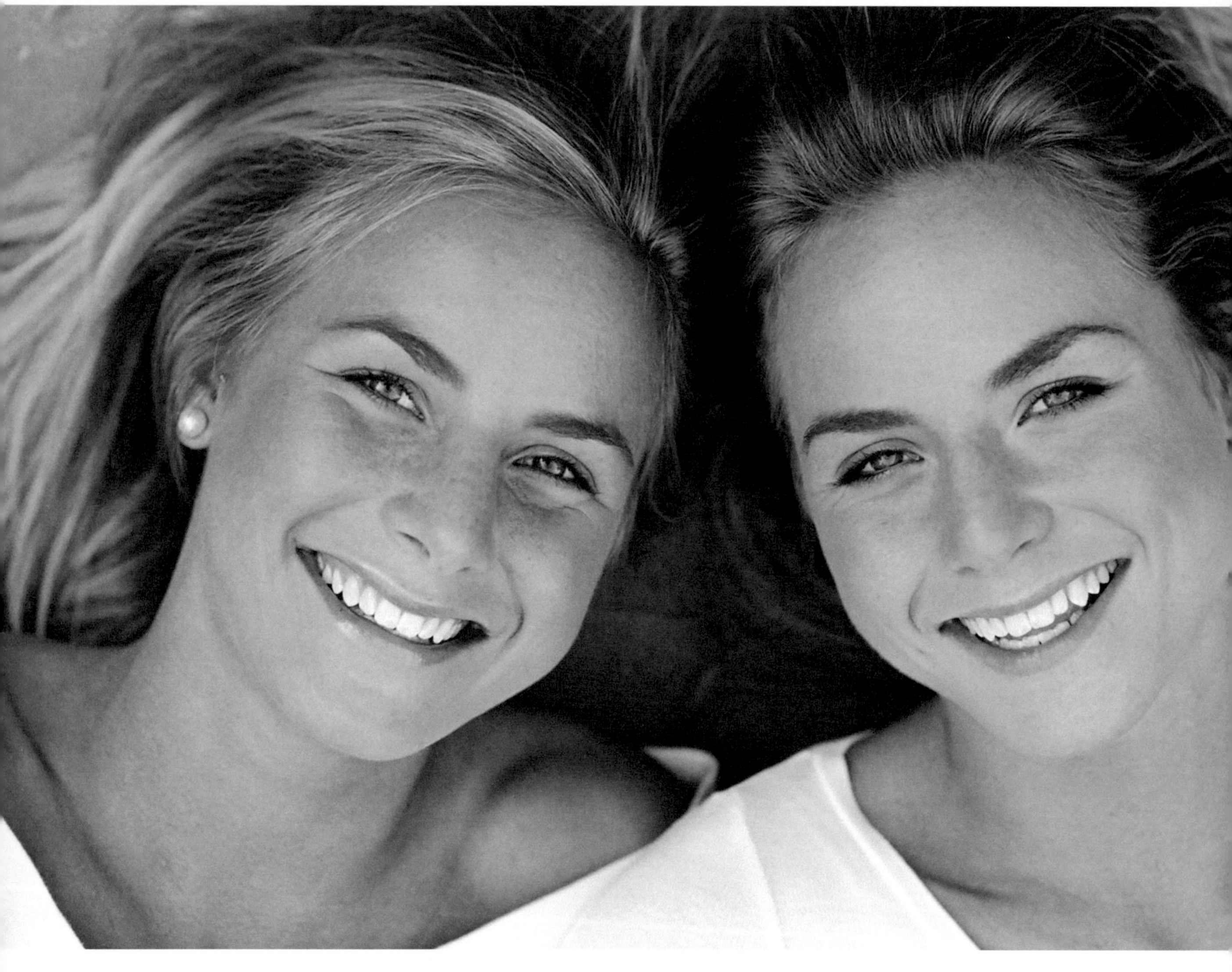

Dreaming with Sister

We missed our stop, pillows
for each other, mouths slumbering wide
to passing worlds, arms loosely hugging
lunch boxes–two lives lolling in time
to a mothering squeak and groan, halt
and roll. The driver followed breathing
to find us in the last seat,
twin strands glistening down our chins.

~ *Derek Sheffield*

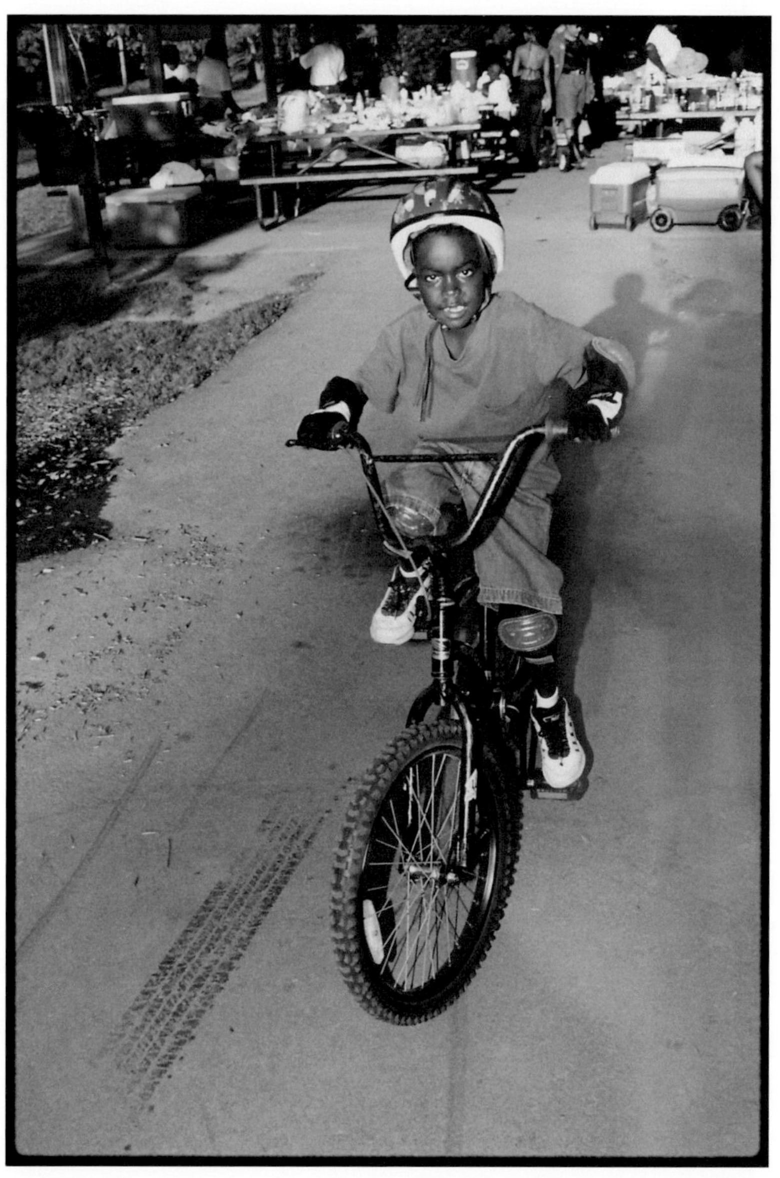

Letting Go

January 4; 70 degrees. I smell snow melting.

My son and I are renewing our warm-weather ritual–
he rides his bike, as I walk, through our neighborhood.

Tall and trim, with a receptive mouth and defining brown eyes,
Andy's the kindest eight-year-old I know.
We've done ride-walks since he was four.

Our method aims to be clock-tick regular.
The route is a circle. I point the way, he leads.
I plod, he meanders–but waits to cross streets.

Interruptions are few. We stop to watch
two white-tailed deer on a lawn. As we
crest a hill, Andy pauses and says, "Hold me, Dad."
He means, "Steady me," but I do not correct him.

I usually feel quiet, poised, weightless, and connected
to Andy. But today the trees' boney fingers,
lighted by harsh winter sun, suggest less serenity.

Tomorrow is his ninth birthday. Three days ago, Andy
gave up long hair. The crew cut reveals jagged jawbones –
something of a man. His new enthusiasm is building
model planes and aircraft carriers. He wants to fly.

Andy's eyes have seemed to look inward.
Today they look for new worlds to conquer.
He asks to cross the street on his own.

It is time. I let him go.

~ Dan Logan

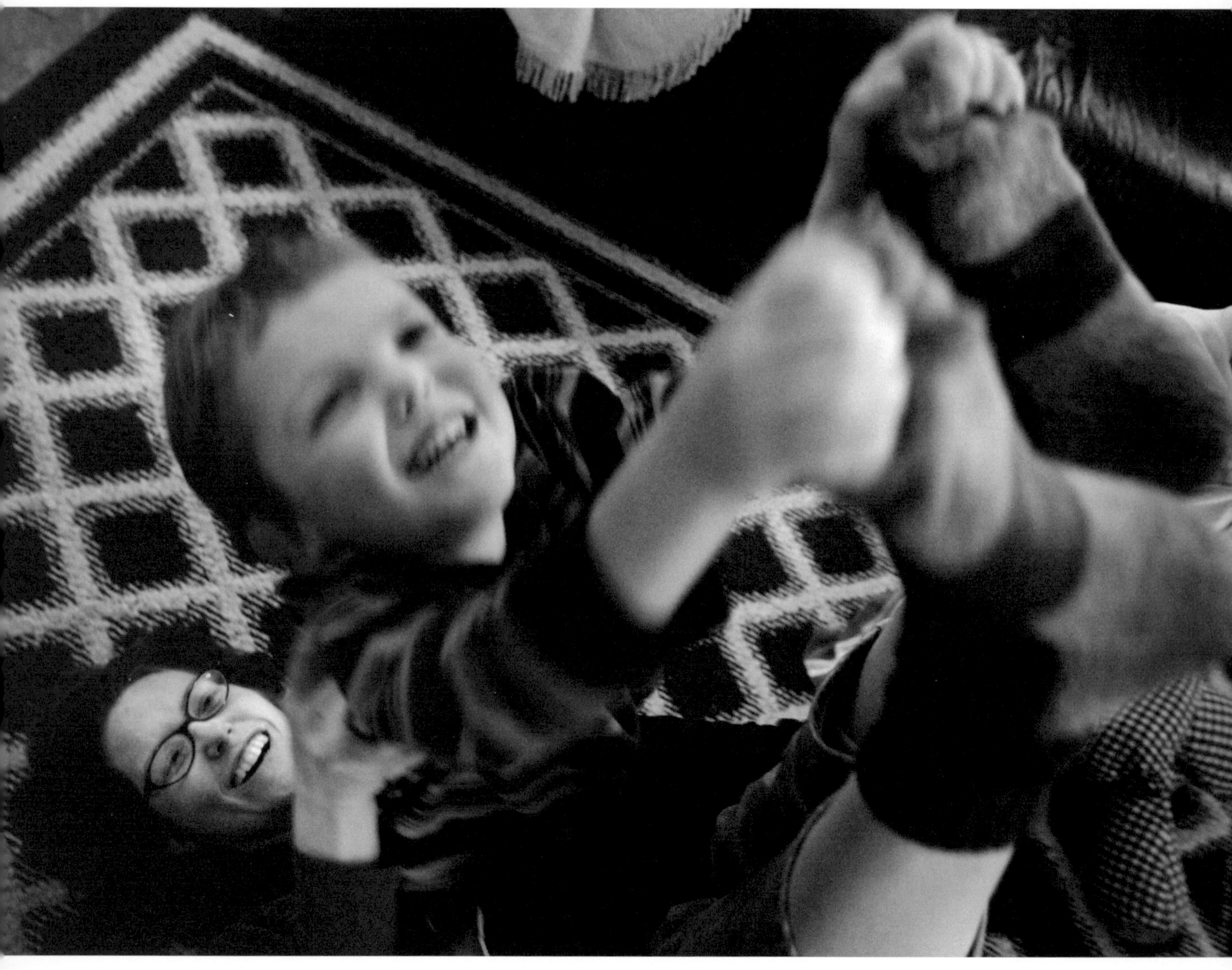

Haiku

my son and i
counting fireflies
counting stars

~ Roberta Beary

Haiku for my mother

Mommy cares for me.
Mommy always forgives me.
Her love never ends.

~ Kyndall Brown (age 12)

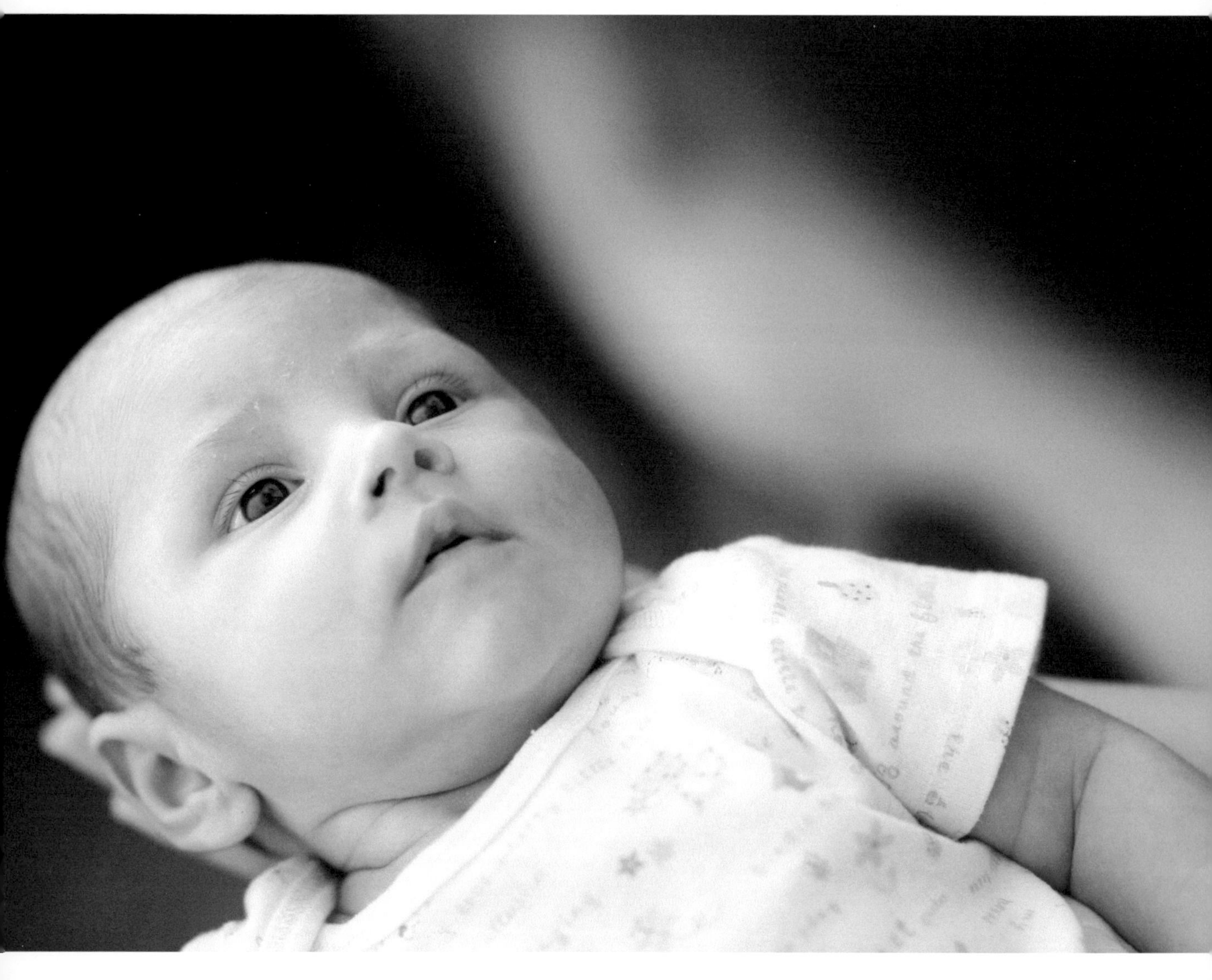

The Oceans of Your Eyes

(for Adem)

You were born in a record-breaking heat wave
that covered New York like a sodden blanket,
trapping us in a caul of our own humidity.

And when you crowned, leonine,
tearing flesh and breaking bone,
you entered this world like a jungle beast.

When I'd given all the blood I had,
enough for two lifetimes,
I held you yawning, wide and keen,
clutching my skin with survival strength.

You were all devouring and sucking smiles
as you balled your elegant fists
and grasped life with all ten fingers.
You kicked the heated air with perfect promise.

And I looked into the oceans of your eyes,
fathomless, infinite and wise,
while I prayed for some liberating imperfection
to guarantee you'd never be a soldier

~ *Adele C. Geraghty*

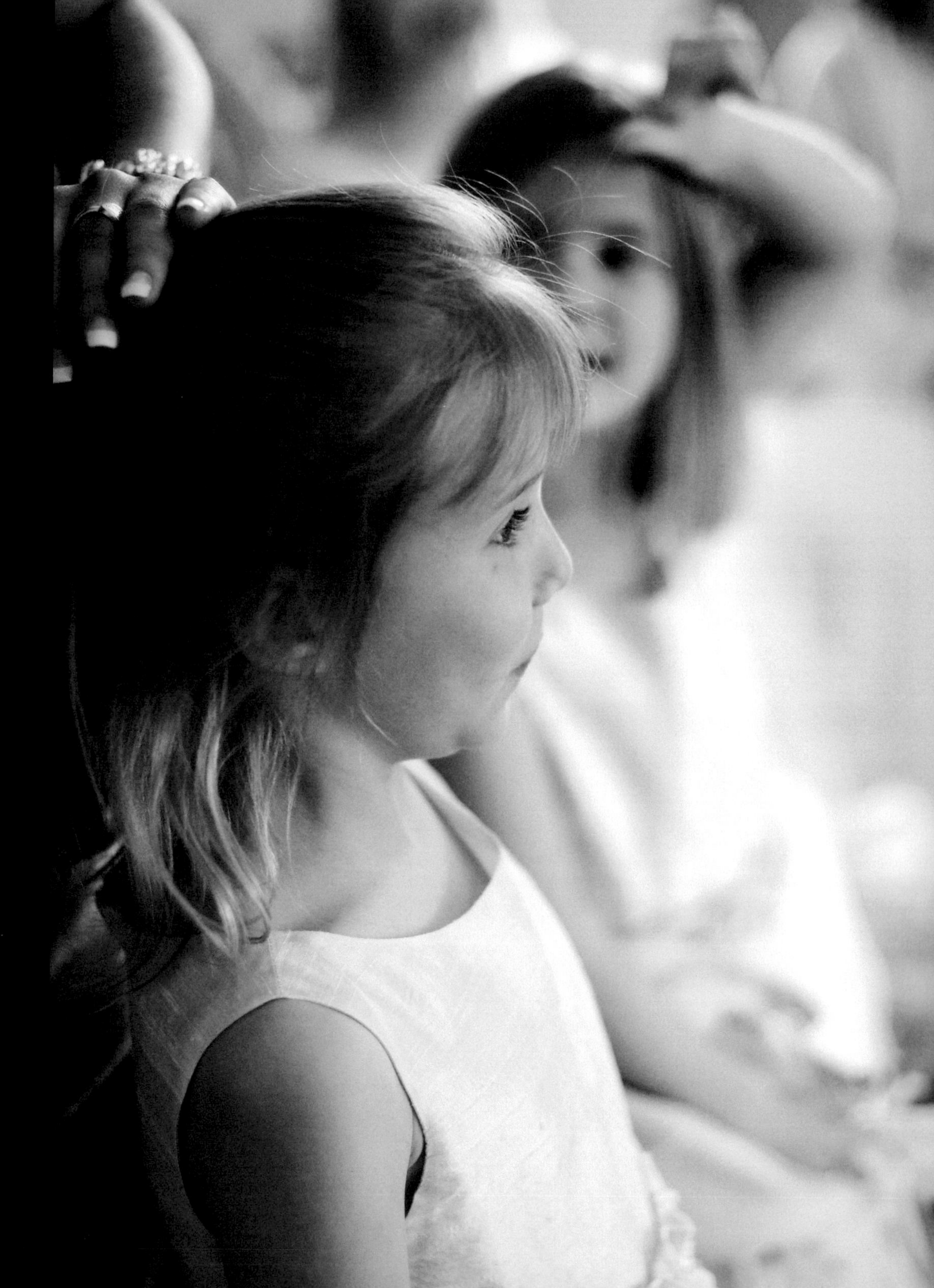

Braiding

I stood between her knees,
locked into place so I couldn't squirm
as she pulled each triple-strand hank
eye-wateringly tight, lest wayward wisps
work their way out of the proscribed pattern.
Left over center, right over center,
always the outside coming across
to become itself the center. With each crossing
she wove into my head with Germanic precision
a preference for order over chaos, then added
the incongruity of bright, ironed, grosgrain ribbons.
At length, released from the prison of her legs,
I went, braided, into the world, bound
to her as strongly as though by ropes
or that severed cord that once made us one.

~ *Gretchen Fletcher*

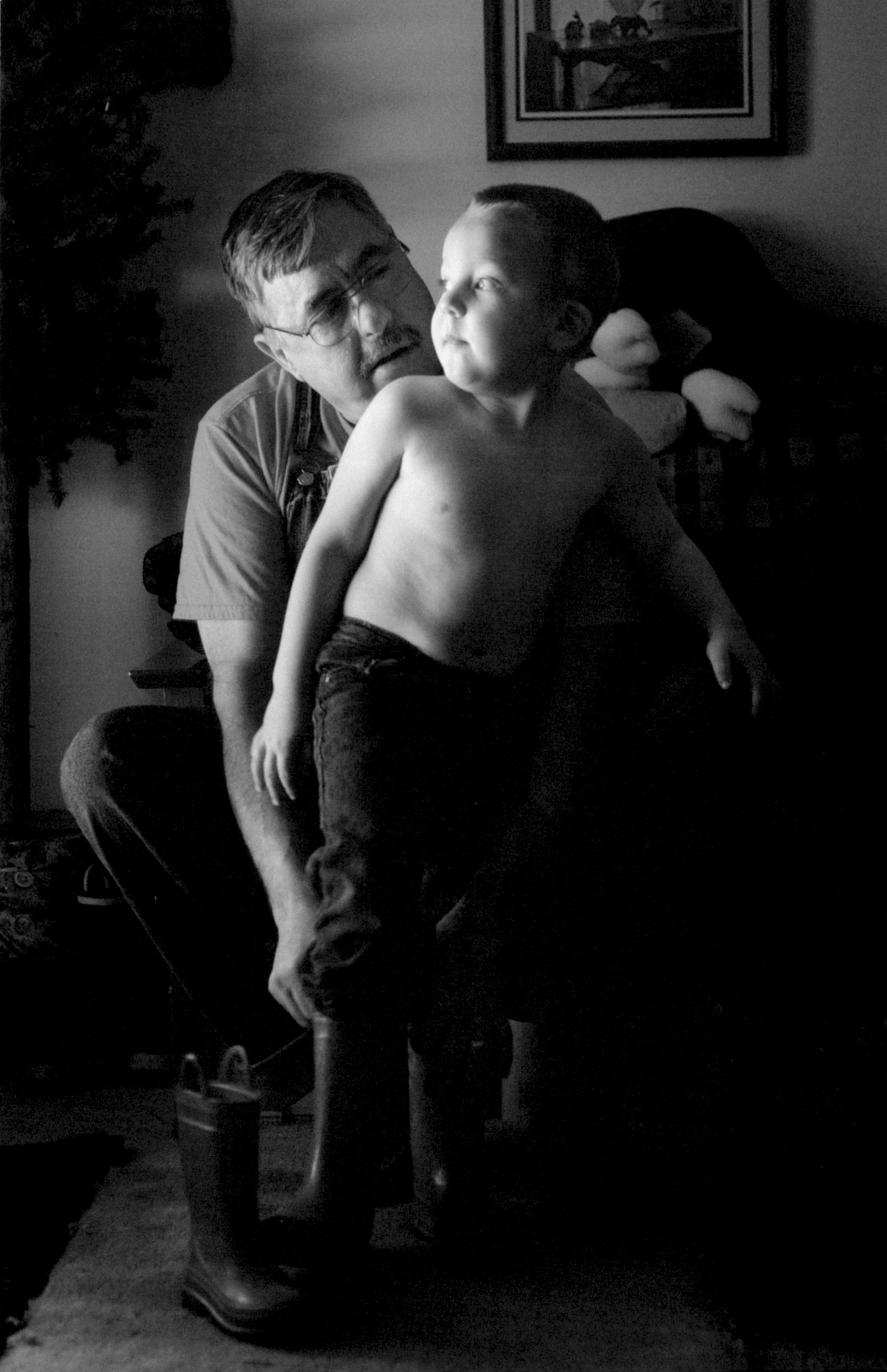

Overalls and a Starched White Shirt

He was overalls and a starched white shirt
buttoned to the neck,
slippers on Sunday with a biscuit shine,
halo of soft white hair,
pair of broken wire-rimmed eye glasses
with a string twisted round his ear,
folding money in his bib,
rattling money in his pocket.

He was brogans and flannel shirt weekdays,
bull tongue plow,
expert on the rear end of a mule,
on hunkering and squatting in a garden,
on slaughtering a hog or birthing a calf.

He was a ladder-back chair
on a broken down porch,
iron bed with a chenille counterpane,
woodstove in the kitchen,
armload of kindling,
water bucket, slop bucket, feed bucket,
rusty dishpan of chicken feed.

He was a Brumby rocker, his favorite chair,
trunk that held his dead wife's Sunday hat
for more than 30 years.
He was mama and daddy to my mother,
his little girl,
smile from ear to ear.

He was the family Bible
bound with an inner tube from a blown out tire
to keep loose pages from falling out,
the blessing at mealtime,
the prayer at night.

He was a little black book of pencil scratching,
secret loans to family and friends,
Indian war dance,
treasury of scary stories
about witches and ghosts,
bloody bones and scratch-eye,
book of remedies for warts and gout.

He was the messenger
who came to me with a radiant face
hours before my mama died,
told me that she would soon journey
to her heavenly home
to be with him and the family there,
and that I would be all right.

Never a frown, never a scowl,
never an angry or unkind word,
my granddaddy
was a saint
in overalls and a starched white shirt.

~ *Judy Lee Green*

Leo, at Ten who Lived in a Boxcar with Four Sisters, a Brother, and his Mother

He lived on half-time, without romance,
on the edge of railyards, memorized stars
beneath half-moons; he lived on chalk dust
and god, dirty rice and beans, when he could

get them, used shoes were his savior. A drifter,
he chased trains for the hell of it, jumped
off bridges, never learned to swim. He held
fire when he dreamt of his father, a pool

hall statistic; he lived with secrets.
He lived the dream of every black man.
He lived with a bible; he lived without god;
he lived on a corner with cigarettes,

his mother's street smarts, his brother's cool,
his sisters' dreams of getting high off the moon.

~ *Metta Sáma*

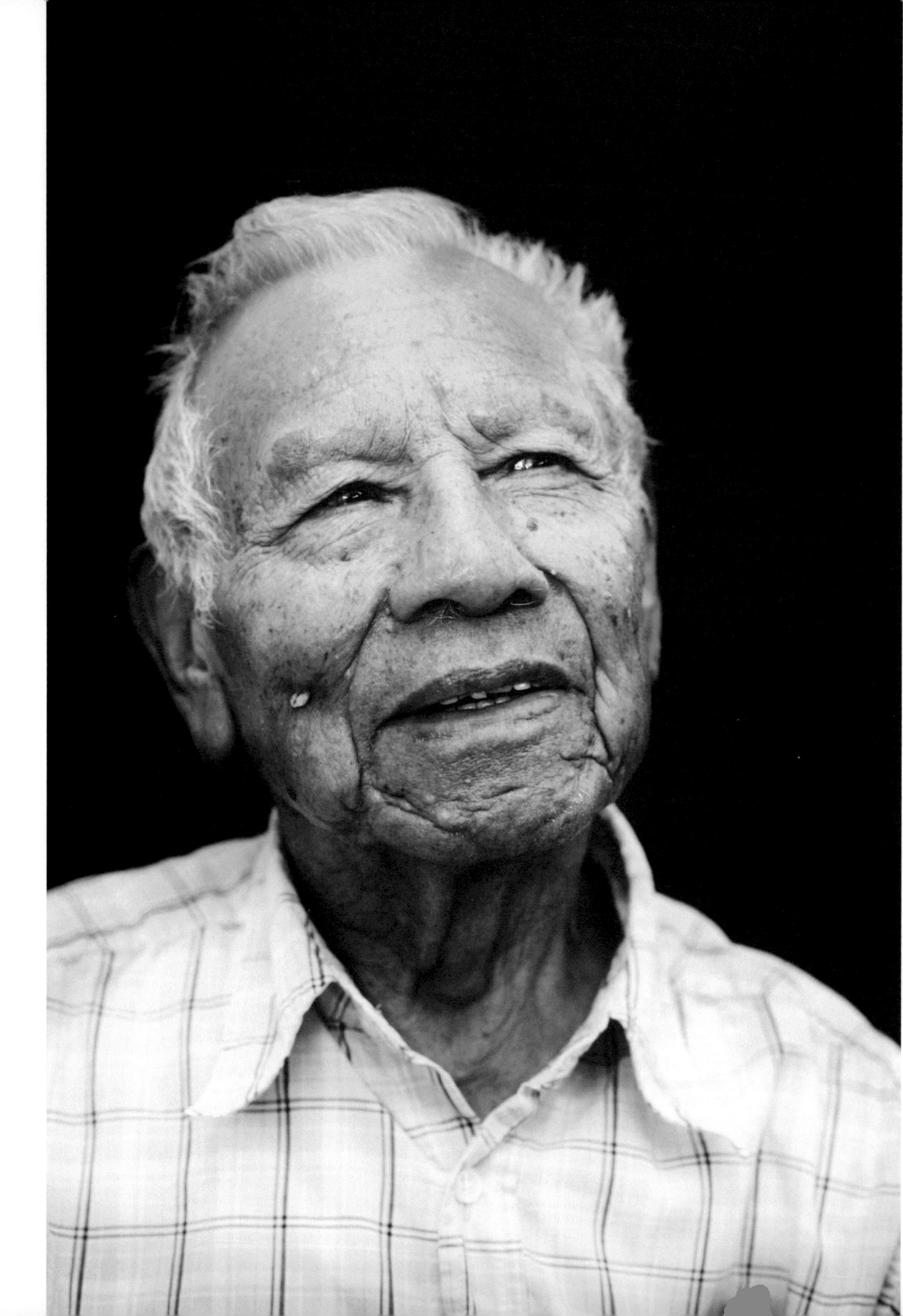

Last Days

for my father

What do you do when the hands don't work anymore?
Early morning awakening to the buzz and fizz of curled wrists.

When your body is no longer the body you've come to love?
Shunt replacement, back surgery, an out-of-date tuxedo.

How to stand it when you stand back from the chair and a slight sway
tumbles into a free-fall, edge-lit against linoleum

where you wait for your daughter, cousin in Florida, Josephine Steele,
someone to call, come in, unfold your legs; scold so who is in charge here?

Not the heart with its blocked valves, not the blood
laced in cumadin, nor the brain straining for the music of Blue Hill Avenue.

Emma noodling past midnight on Devon Street, band tunes
snapped out in wisps of fingers now re-shaped by calcified bones.

You resent each slow click along the industrial floor,
prescribed evening walks down green hallways.

You try to make hospital food taste like home: ginger, garlic, sesame seeds –
uncover the closet of locked plastic urinals, sweet contraband

hidden from the patients who flood sheets, pants, the nurse's
humorless shoes. How to withstand the outrage of old age?

Smile and the world smiles back, you said. I send you my Amen
as long as our bodies still bend, just as long as we both pretend.

~ *Susan Rich*

Trimming the Tree

All the presents
   we forgot
   are here now.
We'll name everything we love:
birds
   unafraid
   to go unanswered,
the river
   flowing
   just beyond our sight,
small stars
   shining without knowing
   what is light,
pencils of sound
   where
   every soul is written,
each branch
   a favorite child,
   in a match
   no one would make.
Now we'll
   point through the dark
   to see memory.
What shall we call it?

~ *Grace Cavalieri*

Chanukah

On the last night, we squeeze
the candle-lighting between my work
and the children's Christmas shopping spree.
We recite the blessing in Hebrew, a language
none of us really knows. The flames
reflect along Pyrex tubes; their glow diverts us
from the wad of caulk I used
to mend the glass menorah
when it broke five nights ago. We have gifts.
One son reads dumb jokes from his Far Side
calendar; the other scowls at the shirt
I should have guessed he would not like:
cream, with a pocket-slit that flashes purple
on the left side of the chest. The doorbell rings;
the boys are off to get ready
for their father's holiday. I watch
blue pussy willows gutter in nine wax-encrusted cups
and consider the miracle of boys
who say the borucha willingly, and by heart.

~ *Judith Strasser*

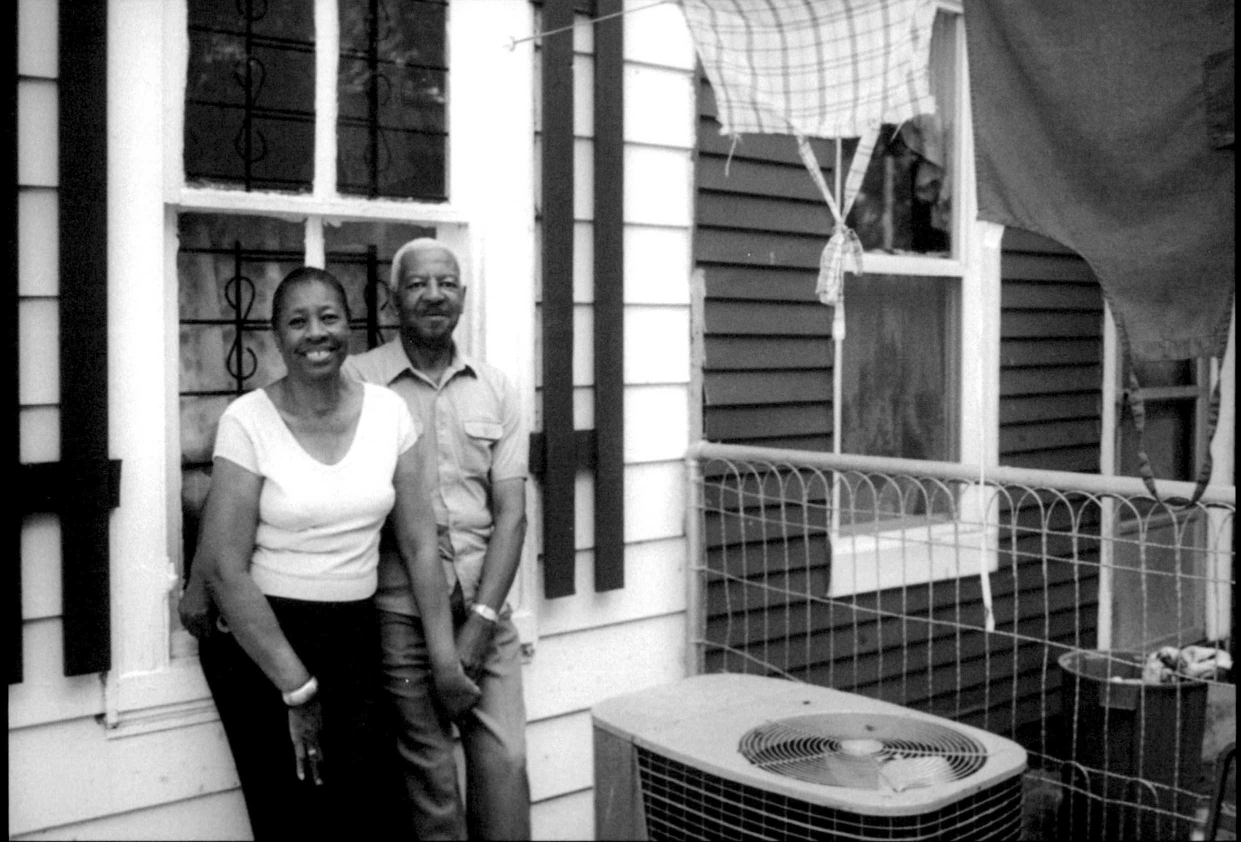

So the Snapshots Say

they had their moments
the two of them afro to afro
on aunt edna's couch,
blushes of courtship
written over their thirty something faces.

tight lips pursed over Kool cigarettes and B.B.'s blues
stretched over the lyrics of Cool Jerk and the 45's
they played after Sunday
dinner;
the giggles when they played Scrabble and gin rummy.

weekday dinners around the formica table
a communion of something hot and homemade with kool-aid;
bread broken over the latest oil bill;
whose teacher had called in a mischief report.

didn't blush as much
when the shudders were off
since divorce was not part of the history
silver and gold anniversaries,
retreat of sleep, r&b reminders,
and us:
plaid pants stuffed with dollar store pampers;
eyes wide watching it all
from the mantle.

~ *darlene anita scott*

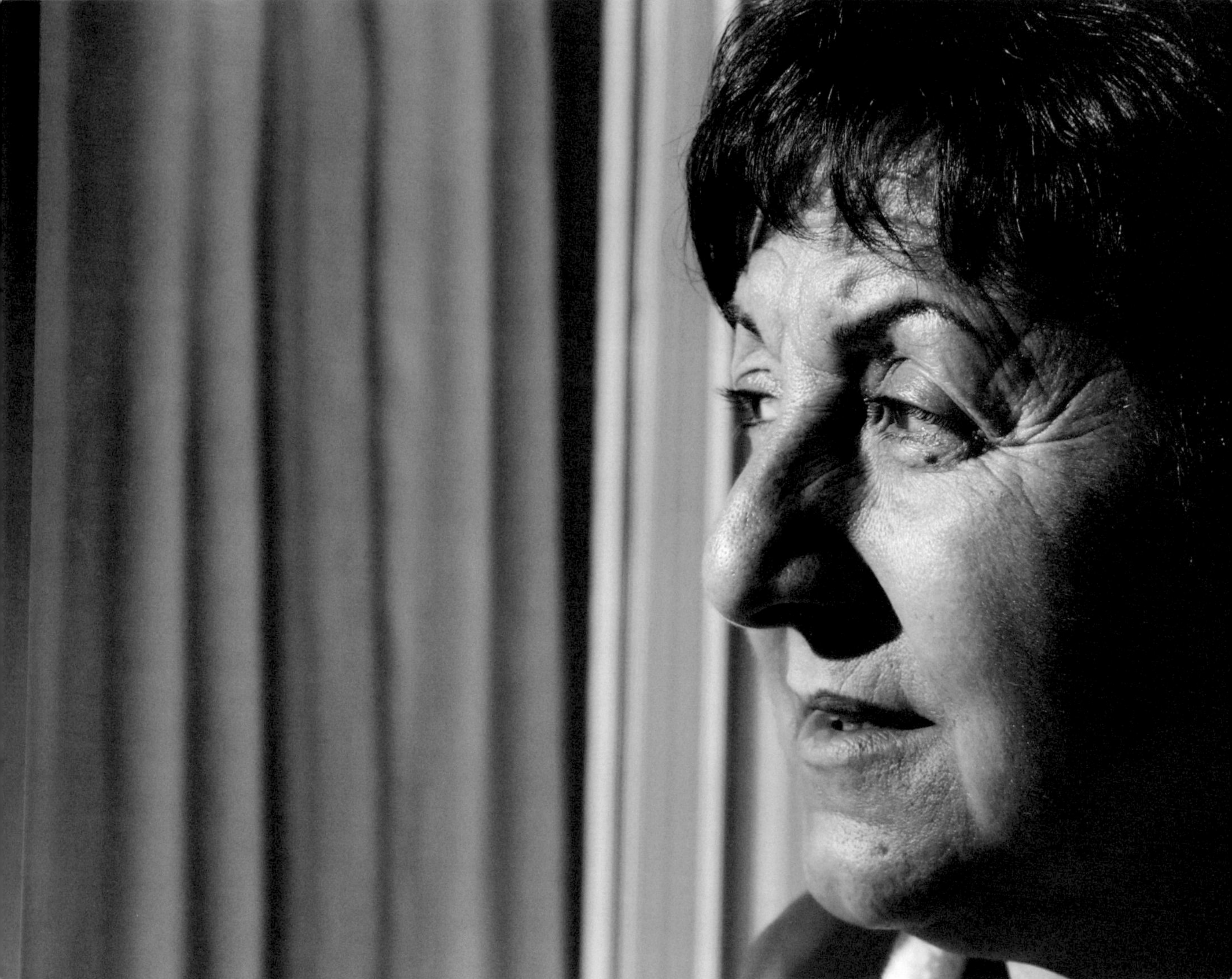

Goddess Redundant

I sit quietly in my rented room in my sons' home,
engaged in my own temporary but neatly decorated surroundings;
bits of a lifetime, winking consolably from every corner.
I am painting water colour vignettes which take the place of smoking,
fingers gripping the paint brush like a fag stem, lusting for a drag.

My music is pierced, left bleeding in staccato tatters,
by raised voices, deliberating the spare room's content.
As oblivious to my listening as they are to my breath,
too busy to dine with me or to meet my friends,
sometimes when finding my room conspicuously empty,
they wonder where I could possibly have gone.

Once, my voice was rapture, holding them in a seated embrace;
it wrapped them in magic trust, deep as blood and lasting as bone.
Their firefly eyes danced, enthralled, inhaling my stories,
swallowing my smiles and vision. Almighty God commanded less allegiance.

There is no patience now with transparent talking and trivialities;
embryonic sentences quickly aborted, too boring to complete gestation,
spit dust-dry and shapeless by a ruined pedestal.
They have declined my invitation to attend my latest performance
and to view my newest painting. They told me to go to my room
while they sort this out, just what to do with a useless old girl like me.

~ *Adele C. Geraghty*

Palette

Her head resting against the malignant white
of the hospital pillow, she chooses colors.
"Bury me in rosy peach?" Mother asks.
"And just a touch...not real
red lipstick." A reminder.
Of what I'm not sure. Still,
I unwrap the present I've brought.
A sketch pad. Colored pencils. A small gum eraser.

The nurse interrupts. Time for lunch.
Lettuce and tomato, baked potato, braised halibut
with lemon. "No grapefruit or oranges back then,"
Mother schools me. "Only at Christmas."
I open the top drawer of the nightstand,
shut my gift of supplies inside.

Back home she has separated
the needles, threads, and thimbles; packed
remnants of dotted swiss, voile and yellow organdy.
In a shoebox, clippings of me and my sister,
our bangs, Dixie-Peached and Saturday -straightened
in Miss Nancy's beauty shoppe; hot combs,
the quick pop fry of a water drop
just missing a lobe of our ears. Later, the slight rattle

of a pot; collards, steam escaping , odors
assaulting our noses; heavy stroked promises
of the next day's delicacies,
real as Mother standing
in the backyard years earlier,
her hands holding a cocoon
up to sunlight, "This will
be a swallowtail butterfly."

~ *Jeannette Drake*

Feeding My Mother at Seventy-two

My mother, half between dreamland and nodding,
Half refuses the insistent prodding
Of hand and fork and all-too bland food, feeding
Her half-baked lies and desperate pleading;

Each triumphant swallow brings me back to days
She missed having abandoned me at birth in a drug haze;
It is my father's mother's hand I remember
Feeding my asthmatic wheeze at two or three,
As I feed her thirty-some-odd years later,

Bent between the gasping glazed guilt of a nod and dream;
As the nursing room window clouds with steam,
My vain words vanish like finger-scrawled letters,
You have to eat so you can get better.

~ *Tony Medina*

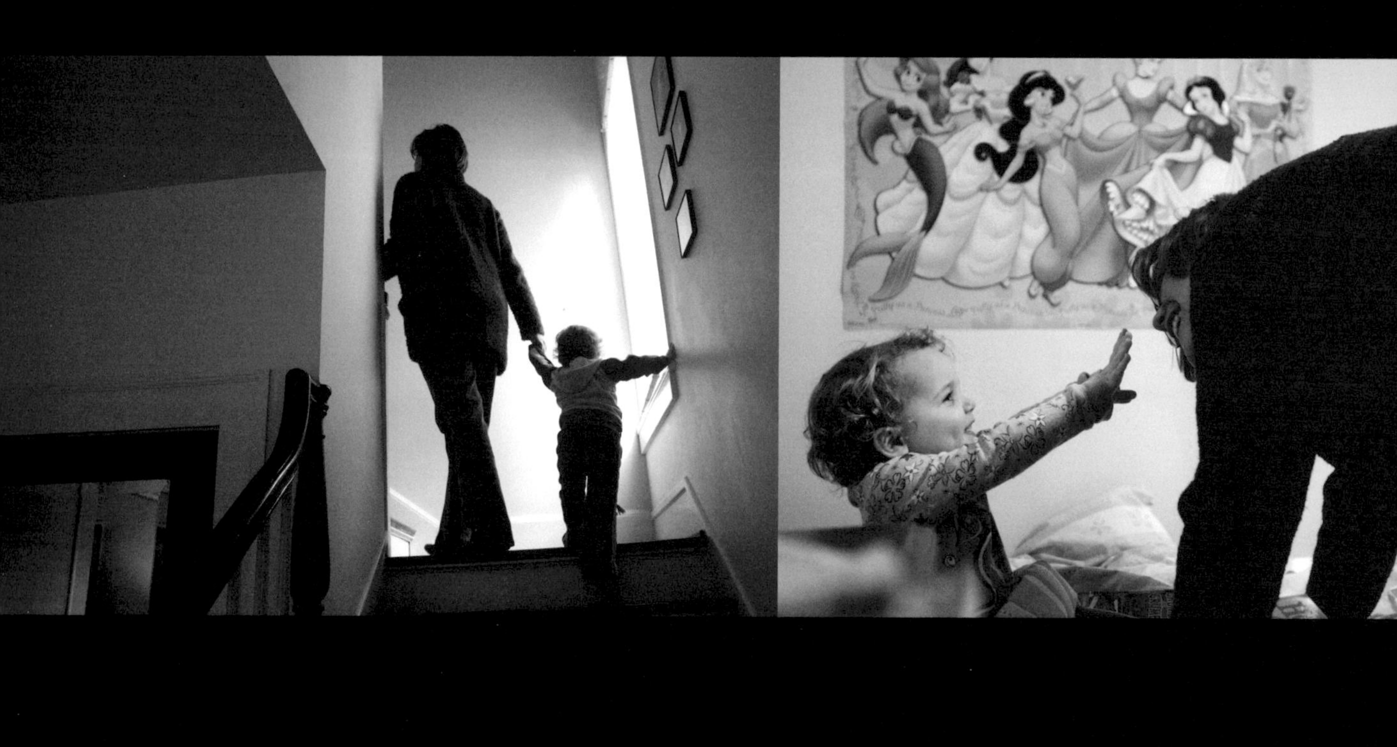

Nighttime Ritual

Sometimes still, our daughter
wants one of us
beside her in bed as she falls

into sleep each evening,
as if she knows
another realm demands

the solitary self,
and so she seeks
this small favor –

companion across the threshold,
solace for the journey in.

~ *Andrea Potos*

He is, She is

4 September 2007

They are the cradle in which we rest
They are the teachers of life's tests
They are God's Angels who hold our hands
They are the pedestal upon which we stand

He is the strength that resides in our souls
The mental power that makes us whole
He is the belief that we can fly
And the discipline when we've gone too high

She is supreme ruler of beauty's regime
She is the beacon through which love can be seen
She is the patience that we grow to acquire
The richness that quenches a child's desire

He is reality when life's not fair
Possibility and hope in times of despair
He is the rhythm behind our talents
Keeping us steady; keeping the balance

She is the silence between the notes
The honest thought behind paint brush strokes
She is the ink of a scholar's page
Introducing the creativity we spiritually crave

They hold the seeds from which we grow
And share the wisdom that we must know
They are the confidence, built deep within
The trust that inspires us to speak this again and again

They are the parents of the world

~ Noni Carter (Age 16)

To My Daughter on a Fine Fall Day

I stand behind you and push,
harder and harder.
You pump higher.
Feet kick the air.
You swing back,
just miss my arms
waiting to receive you.
Hands fall to my sides,
hide themselves in coat pockets.

You're over the sandbox,
filled now with maple leaves.
Shoes skim the hedge,
reach past this boundary line.
You lie in your bed of air,
no pillows for your head.

I watch you wake,
hanging there above me,
a sparrow in its nest.
Your fingers clutch the chains,
probe the links,
let go the hold.
You jump, splitting the noonday sun.
I cannot stop your feet from touching ground.

~ *Carol Carpenter*

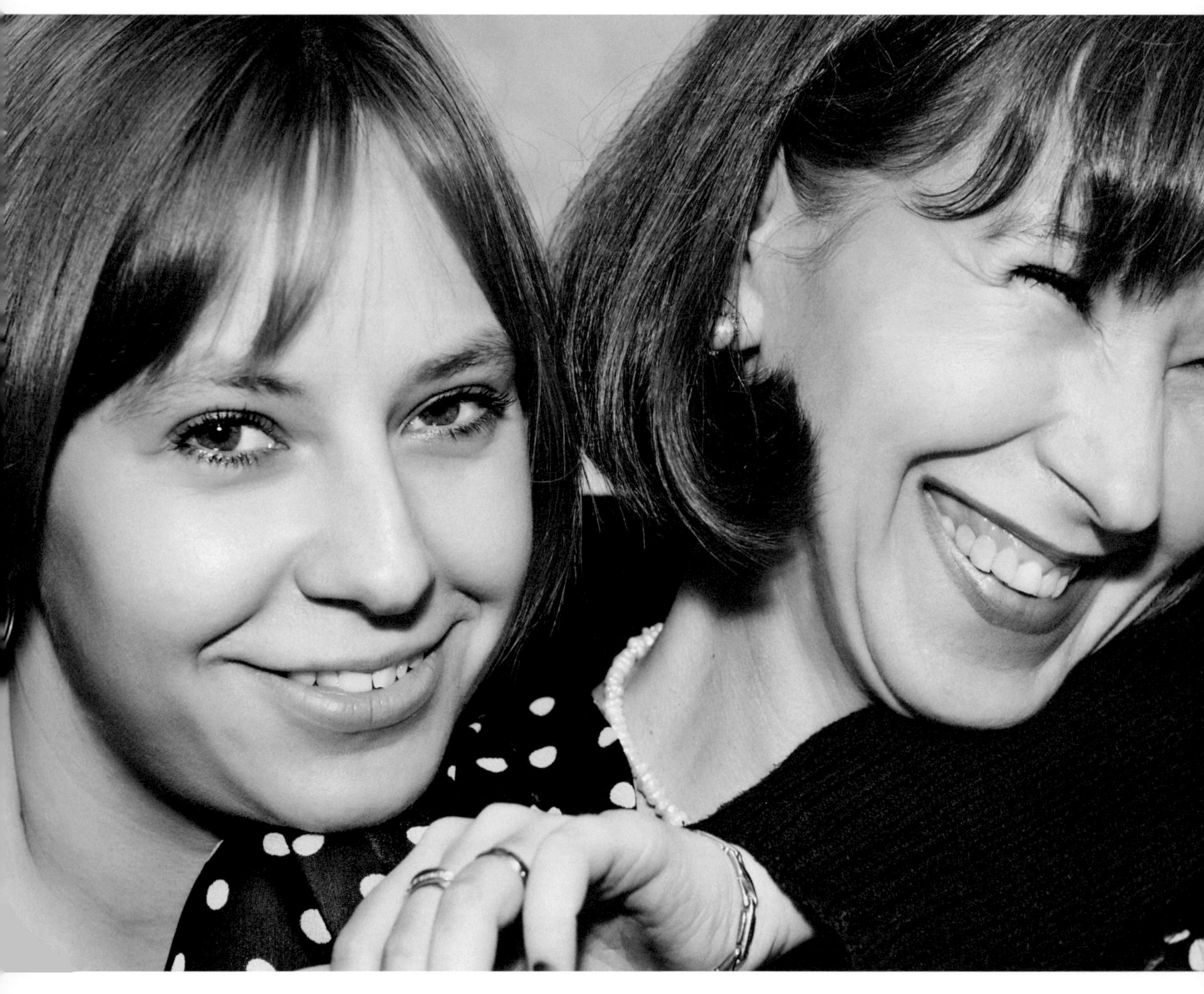

Mother, Daughter

today I'm 29,
and we laugh

like girls inside a homemade fort
eating ice cream

about my birthdays adding up
and hers subtracting

in 14 years we will both be 43

~ *Shana Yarborough*

Haiku

there wd be no poems
without the childhood joy   the
playful way u loved

~ *Kwame Alexander*

Between Them

This is the mother.
This is the daughter.

Between them turns the morning
soft light filtering through

the matchstick shades, the unlived day
in the still pond of the sleeping

girl's room. Here: the mother holds
her breath, pausing time as if

it did not consist of inexorable waves.
Here: a trajectory cupped in the new curves

of hips under quilt.
Don't break

the spell, don't start
the clock, don't wake the child-woman.

She rests a hand between the daughter's
shoulder blades. Porcelain-thin wings,

not yet thick with years, rise, spread,
and fall, rise, spread and fall.

~ *Sarah Conover*

Home for the Holidays

Holidays were not convenient.
Packing, cramped hours in the car,
the lumpy sofa bed in the basement,
prickly kitchen chitchat.
As I cut carrots for salad,
Mother mentioned
the length of my son's hair,
my daughter's table manners,
the unraveled hem on my dress,
the right way to peel carrots.
Her love had a fixed shape, like
cranberry sauce fresh from the can.
I learned to truss my lips,
identify with the turkey
squeezed into a rigid steel pan.
Smothered in spices,
basted every thirty minutes –
turkeys were pampered in her house.
Exactly what I miss now
in this more convenient time of life,
when I can flip through my phone book
and invite other motherless middle-aged couples
for turkey, whole cranberries, and polite conversation.
No words of advice, suppressed squabbles, or love.

~ *Jacqueline Jules*

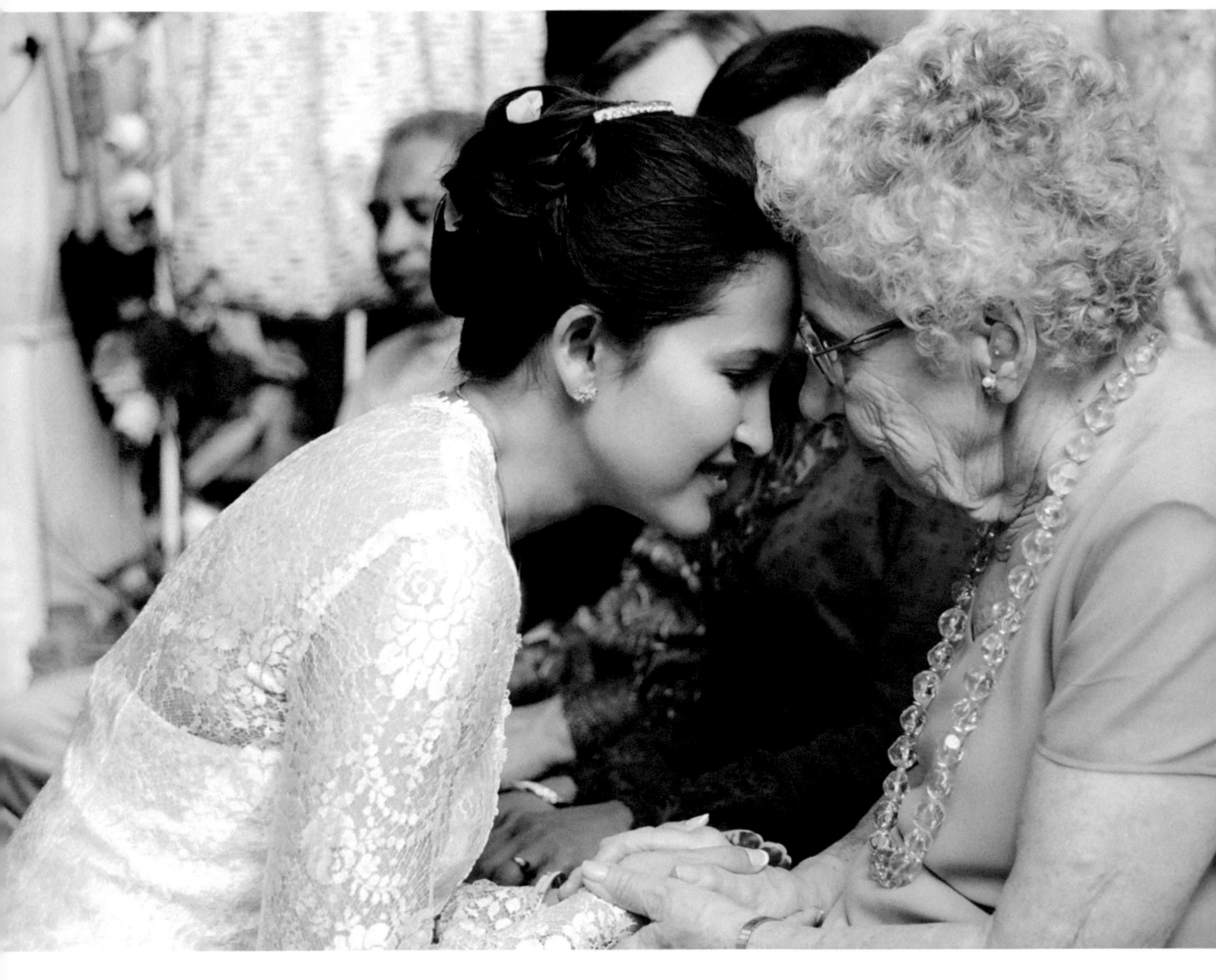

Grandma

watched
the bloody liver
of a calf
quiver in her hand,

washed greens and dishes
till her palms
shriveled,

rubbed fresh butter
on grease burns,
vicks salve
on a small chest,

dug flour
from her fingernails
every night.

her offspring gone,
she nurtured theirs,
though her fingers
cracked and bled.

we saw her smile,
never knew she dreamed
of manicures,
piano keys,
the sweet skin
of a lover's back.

~ *Matilda Cox*

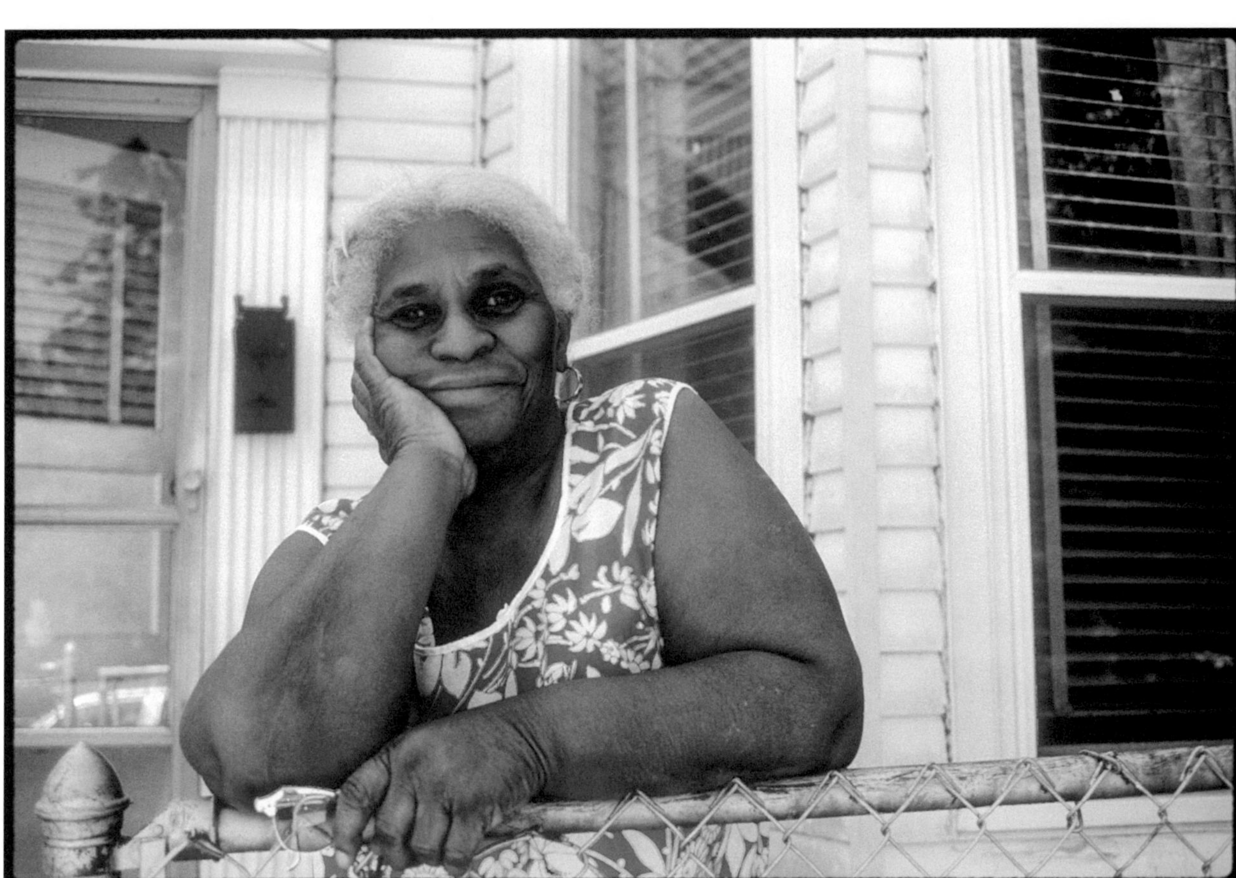

Dizzy

I woke up 3 times tonight
with your face on my mind
like a song that set up residence
in my head.

I dreamt of you three times this week
each time I woke up on an airplane
going in different directions

each flying to a place
i say is my home.

I grew up in the Far East,
I mean, Philadelphia
an Orient of coffeeshops and Chinese diners
and when I say I'm disoriented, I am–

I say, meet me on Market Street
and then I realize that's an ocean away
or that the Market Street outside my window
is not the one
I grew up on

Every time you call me there's an echo on the phone
like shouting across a canyon
I woke up on a bus today
staring up at the clouds
like I could walk on them

Your face in my dreams is an echo too,
indistinct and staticky
Disorientation: the loss of the East
broadcasting your voice.

Hold that thought, Grandmom,
I'm coming home soon
all I gotta do is cross
the 3000 miles of dead air
they call the Heartland

~ *Matthue Roth*

Light

Flying from Lisbon to Rome I sat next to
one of those short, elderly ladies in black
who live up to every Portuguese stereotype–
she even pulled out a rosary for takeoff–
and because she fit my expectations

so perfectly, I loved her immediately.
So when we were served
milk for our coffees in foil-lined packets
and she leaned over and placed
one papery, liver-spotted hand on mine

asking, *Açucer?* I wanted so sincerely
to help that the word in Portuguese
flew out of my mind.
I moved my hands as if milking a cow.
Ah! she brightened. *Leite!*

Of course! Pronounced like light.
She brought me to my childhood kitchen,
where my own grandmother left out
a glass of milk for me each day
that shone so brightly in the morning sunlight

that the milk reflected a halo against
the wall behind it, a half-moon
of fulfilled expectation, and I would stand
on that tan linoleum blinking,
struck dumb with happiness.

~ *Kim Roberts*

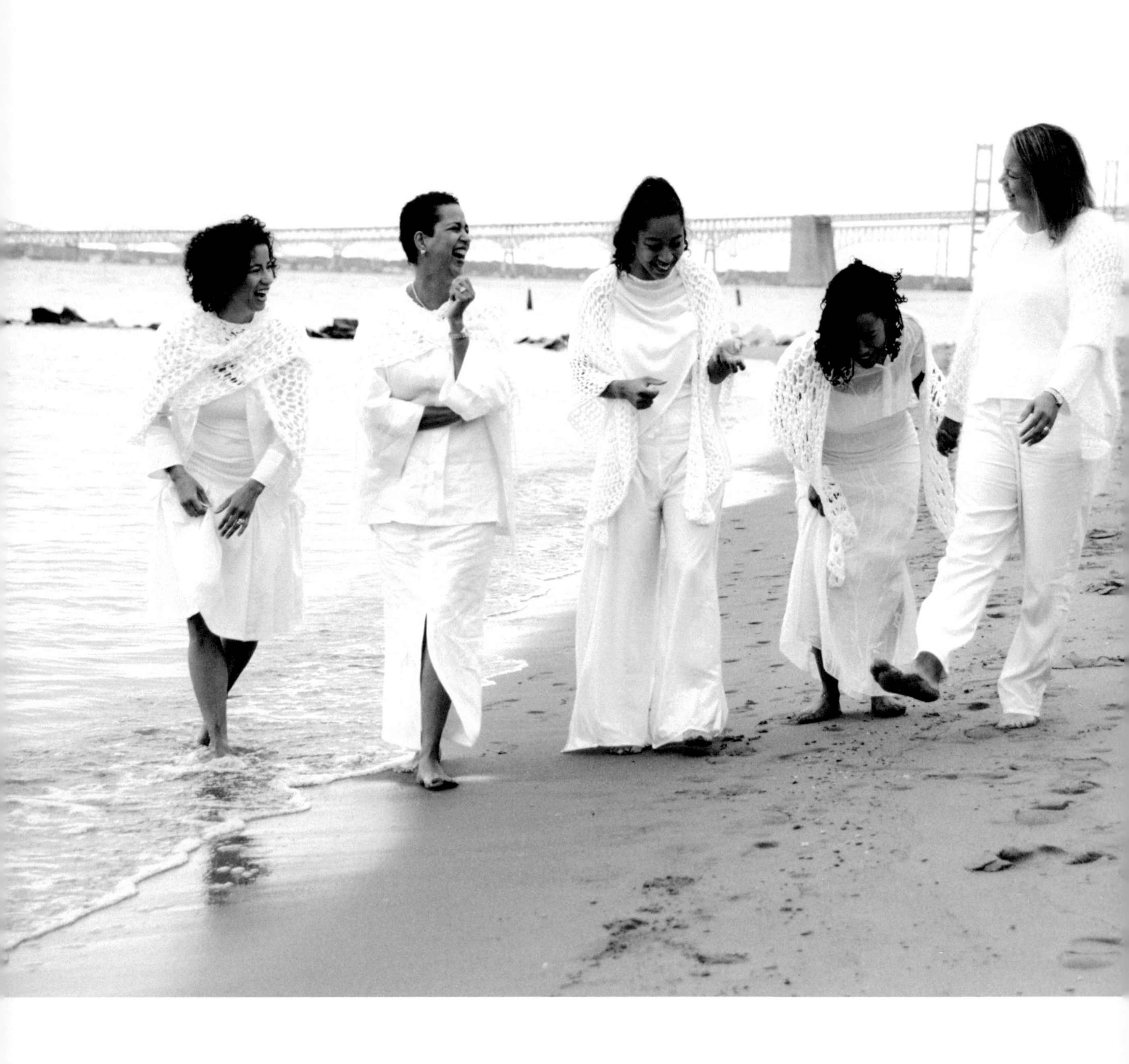

Good Girls

We were the good girls.
Respectful, polite and courteous
with enough please and thank you's
to choke Miss Manners

We washed the dishes, made our beds
did housework and homework on weekends
while the wild girls had all the fun.

We heard their adventures
on Mondays by the bleachers
and wished we'd been wild too.

But our families and our futures
depended on us to be sensible
and serious; to forego
girly pleasures and focus
on the lessons life would teach.

So we saved ourselves
for the right one, who'd
make the waiting worthwhile.

They came and went:
men, their love; jobs and money
never quite living up to our expectations.

We were the good girls
but good was never really good enough
Our lives have left us wishing
we'd been wild.

~ *Maritza Rivera Cohen*

In Chaucer's Steps

Chaucer wrote in April
"folk longen to goon on
Pilgrimages..."
Cabin fever, I guess.
In today's vernacular:
Road trip.

Three chicks in a Honda
With a whirring hybrid engine
70's music blasting
Shooting traffic
Like a spitwad in math class.
We are high
Jacked up on laughter
Slamming toasted, dark roasted
Carmalized and Splendarized
Dunkin Donuts coffee.

Speeding south
We curse good riddance to
Fallow fields of shredded wheat
Frosted in powdery white.
Windows rolled away
We embrace the
First bright buds
Apple-green mown lawns
Marvel at crayon colored tulips
Like we're some wrinkled
Bug-eyed alien virgins
Experiencing warp-speed for the very first time.

We'll head back to the barren North
Long before we're defrosted,
But in the meantime,
There's not much in life
Compares with the gift of true friends,
Dashed dreams and some serious agita
A bag of low-fat pretzels and some high-test beer
As the years roll by the open windows
Feet on the dashboard
Eyes on the horizon
April in our souls

~ *Christine Compo*

Sista to Sista

We are made from the same cloth
woven together by a silver thread.
Our spirits have laughed and cried many lifetimes together.
In this life we are sisters.
Tears of joy, tears of sadness
bond the special moments of our lives
We stood strong
sharing dreams and secrets as others
flowed through our lives leaving their footprints on our hearts.
As the years passed, dreams became realities.
What sweet songs sprang forth from your heart,
as I took the pen to make these precious moments last forever

~ *J.J. Michael*

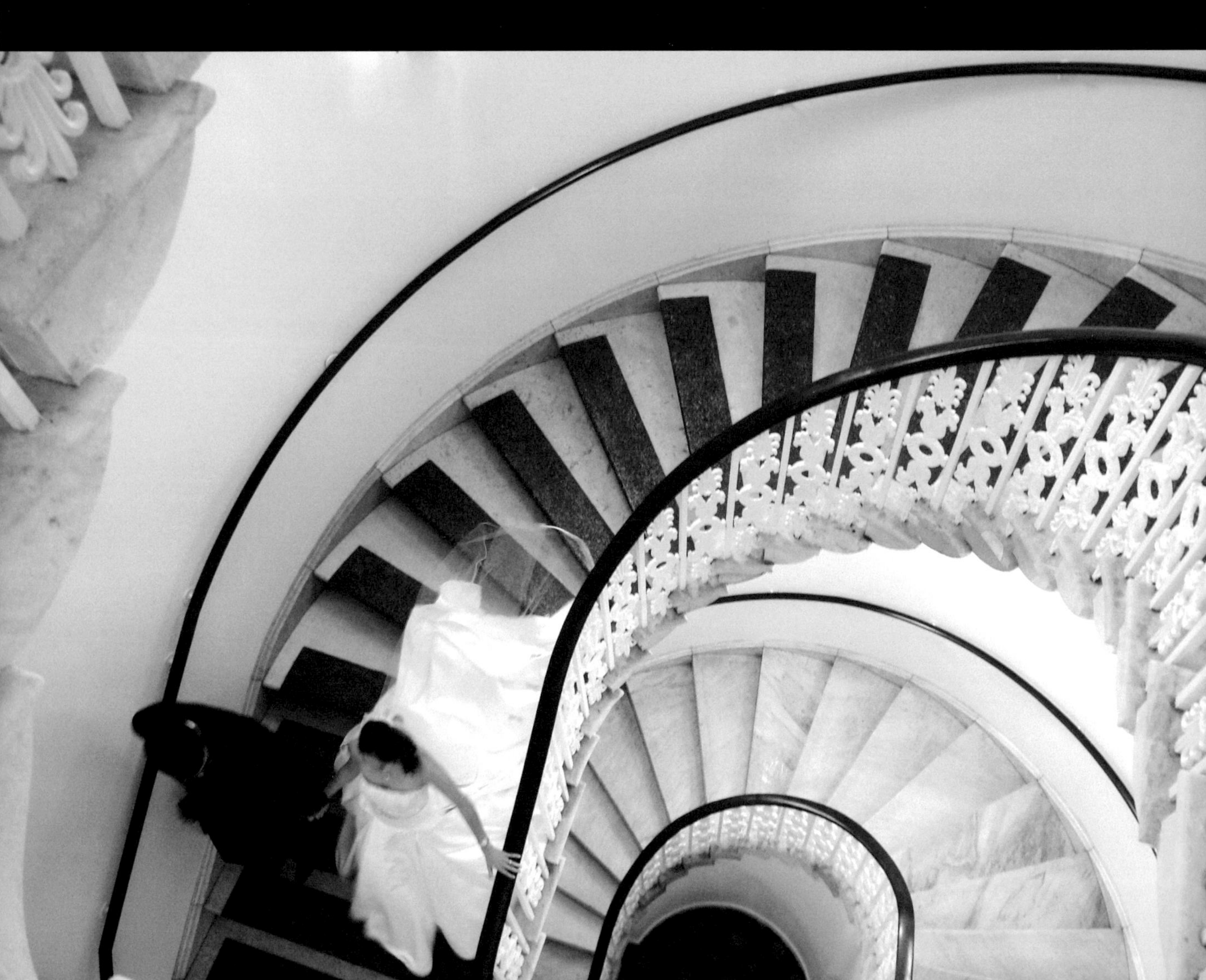

Walk with Me

Can you walk with me
In tune and in time?
Like an August Wilson play
Or a Smokey Robinson rhyme.

Can you walk with me
As I stroll through your mind?
Not in front of me
Nor from behind.

Never becoming parted
By people approaching us,
Confronting our space
And dividing our trust.

Will you walk with me
Be each other's crew?
Holding hands like lovers
As I get to know you.

I'll listen to the concerns
You usually keep confined,
Massage you everywhere
And help you unwind.

I'll be understanding
With eyes that embrace,
Watch over you when you sleep
And dress you in lace.

Protect you in stormy weather
Pull you close to my chest,
If only you'll walk with me
I'll do all the rest.

If you can walk with me
I'll make it worth your while,
Give you life-long pleasure
With one walk up the aisle.

~ *Jason Miccolo Johnson*

Fifty Beads

Fifty years of . . .
weaving
stretching
tearing
mending
every thread locked
still binding to the whole.

Language that has its own language.
A synergy of harmonious difference
both and sometimes not.

There is endurance
in surrender
an invisible ring
shared in bowls of rice
together and apart
incongruent completion
harmony shared through the years
that continues to talk.

A love that most at best
could only wade through.

It is the foundation
and starting point
where we began
the outline that empties
and fills with prayer
a promise that continues
fitting inside the little things that matter.

Togetherness that overshadows first love.

It is perfect imperfection
filtering time into moments
the eye cannot see,
an unspoken thread
holding fifty beads together
some of which we are
a necklace worn in the making
more precious than jewel.
A living love.

~ *Deanna Nikaido*

Family Pictures

(for denise)

We wake up early
Shower separately
I dress in the bathroom
While you look for the iron
In the kitchen closet
For breakfast you have coffee
With light cream
I take Chinese tea with lemon
You brush your hair in the mirror
Place powder and lipstick on your face
I find the belt for my pants

We clean the house before we leave
I empty the trash
Give the cat fresh litter
You wash the four dishes and the one
Cup left in the sink

I stop to watch the plants hanging
In the window
I count the dead leaves

We have lived together for three weeks
Sharing the space within each other
I write in the last pages of my diary
Outside the cars move in different
Directions
Family pictures on the bookshelf
You smile and remind me of what day it is

~ *E. Ethelbert Miller*

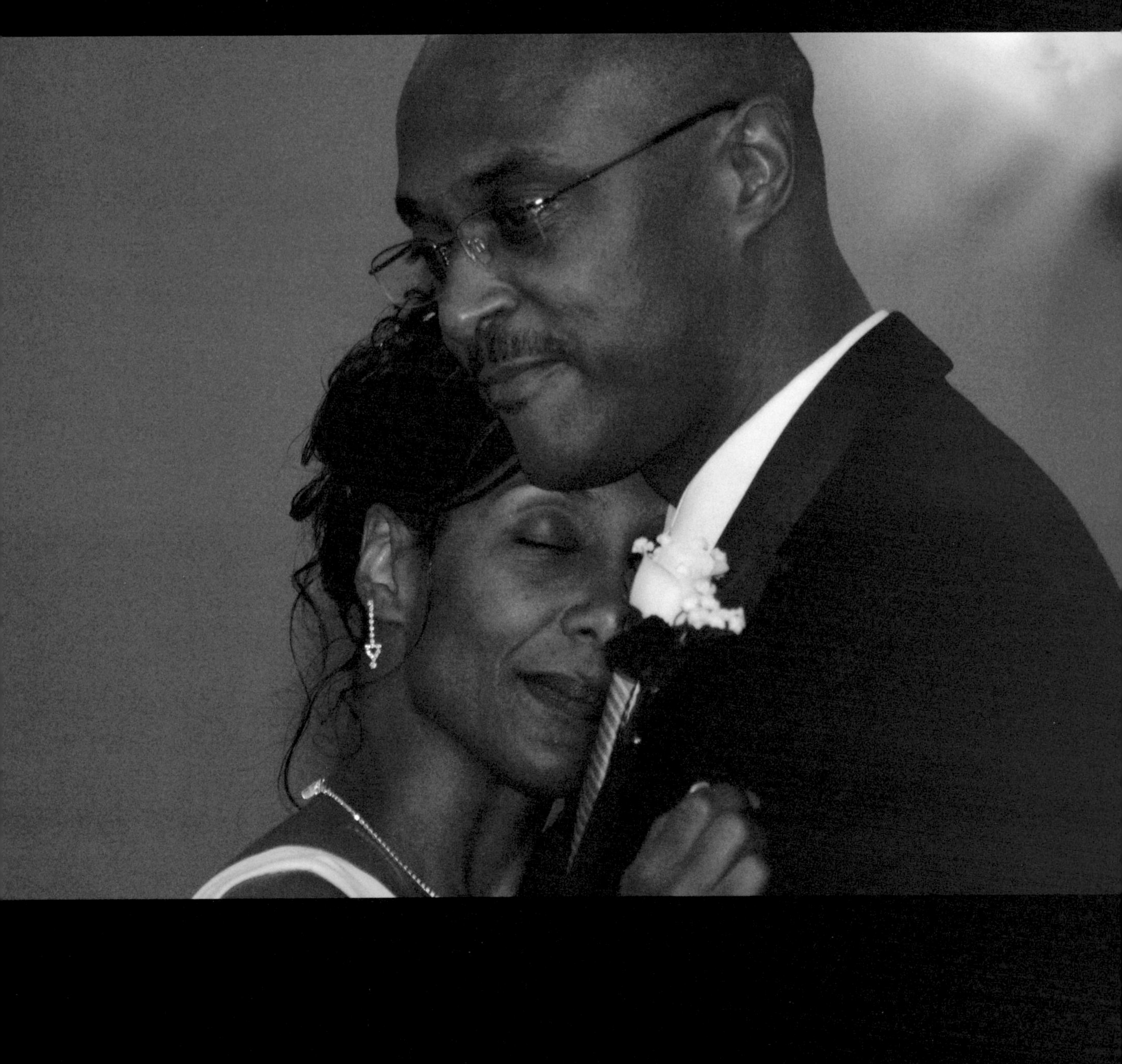

Kupenda

i am not a flamethrower
nor do i drive a red

truck yet at this very moment
i have a burning

desire in the seat of my palm
at the hearth of my

existence to marry you
over and over perhaps

one million times
(recycling the ring of

course) the very thought
of saying i

do over and over
would set my

soul on fire
and i could breathe forever

~ *Kwame Alexander*

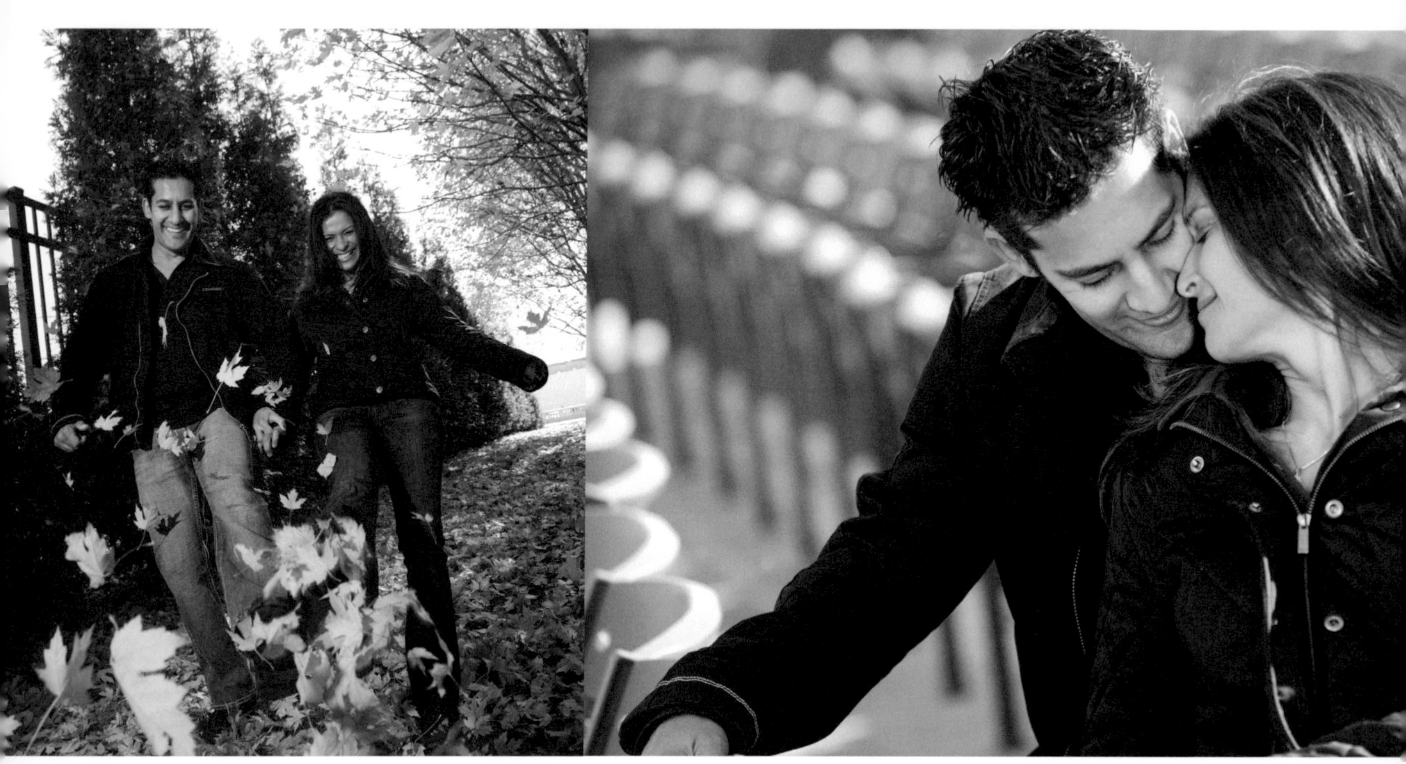

Exploring

Let's take
a Christopher Columbus Day

But first
we need to get
a couple of things straight.

You be the seek
          and I'll be the find.

Hike your fingers
through my forest crown
or let them climb my twin peaks.

Surf my oil glistened skin
          then follow the path

That curves
through hills and valleys
ski the trails

That end tip-toed
          navigate your way North

To discover my gingered-spice.

~ *Sandra Jones*

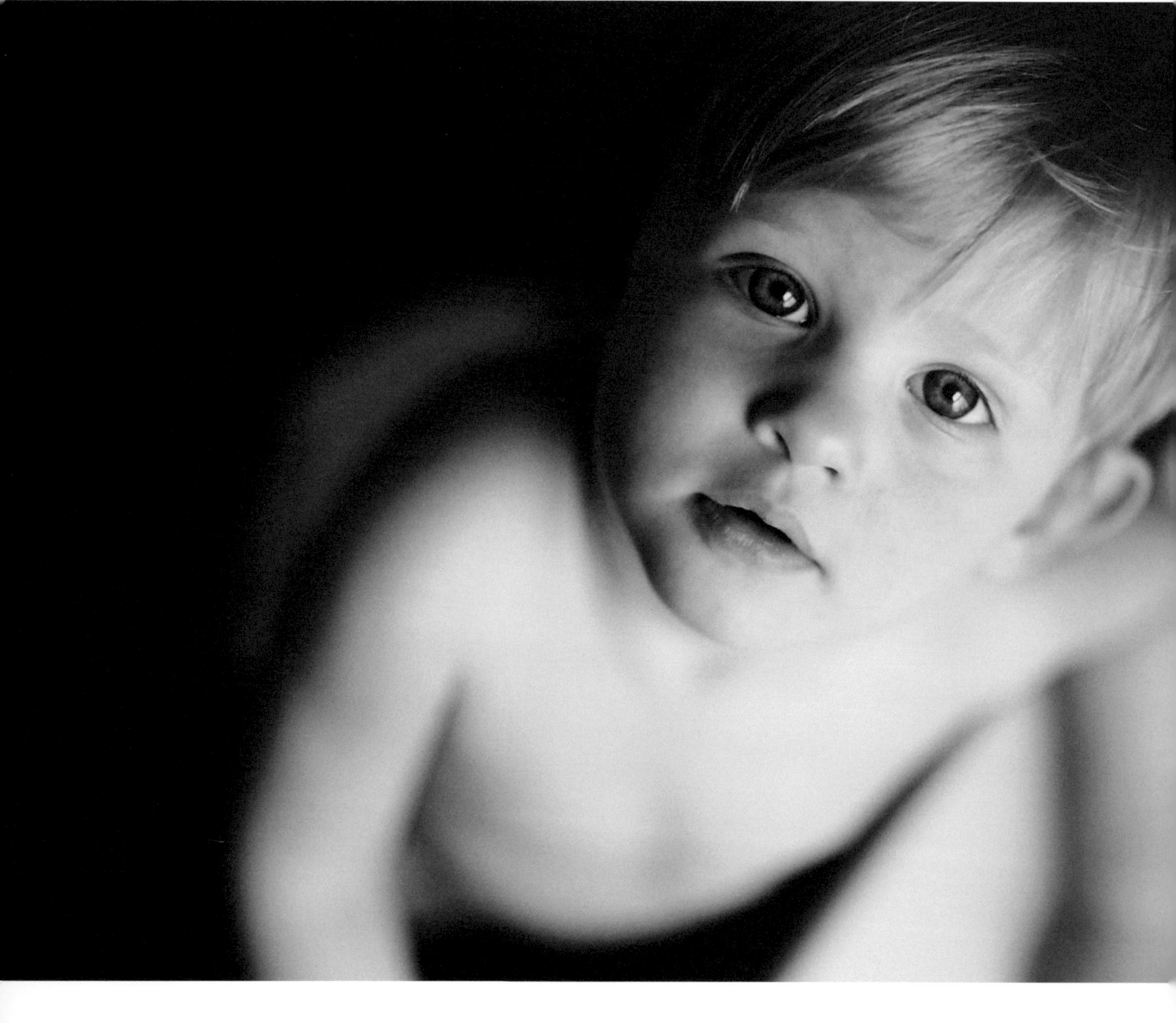

Blond and Agile Child

for Dillon

Your eyes in January are blue
like my best socks, your bottom lip
a place where bubbles gather.
In leap-year February
your mouthy gurgle
hiccups away
my blues. In March
your cooing is something
I'm learning to imitate.
Wild-tempered child, how do you
manage to break
so quickly into blossom
of smile? Your cotton toes
in April
tap a ragtime ditty,
a tune even strangers
soap themselves
with. In May
you ooh-and-aah
like birds calling
for rain.
You take what you like
instead of the given,
you play in June
with a slanted
venetian blind,
and in August,
when your reach
at last exceeds
your grasp, you grab
with glee
for the moon.

~ *Alan Davis*

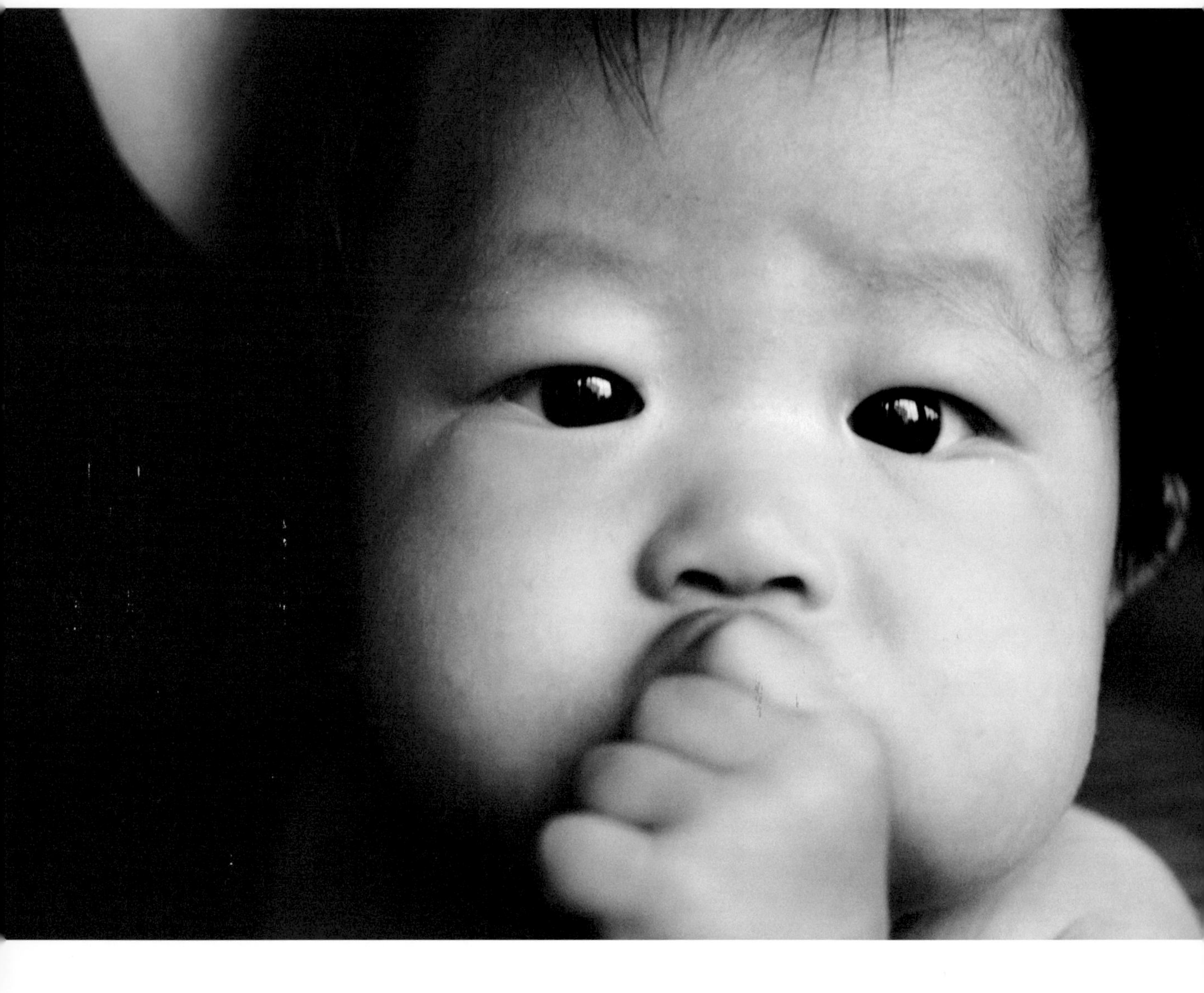

First Born

I did not ask for this:
the bursting pain
the first hiccuping cry
the desolate moments at night,
his drinking lips pressed to my skin.

I did not expect this:
the pangs of dread and regret
the sorrow for all that lay ahead -
slicing skate blade
rugby studs
the craft knife's winking triangle.

I did not want this:
the first beautiful scarlet blood
of my beautiful son.

~ *Christine West*

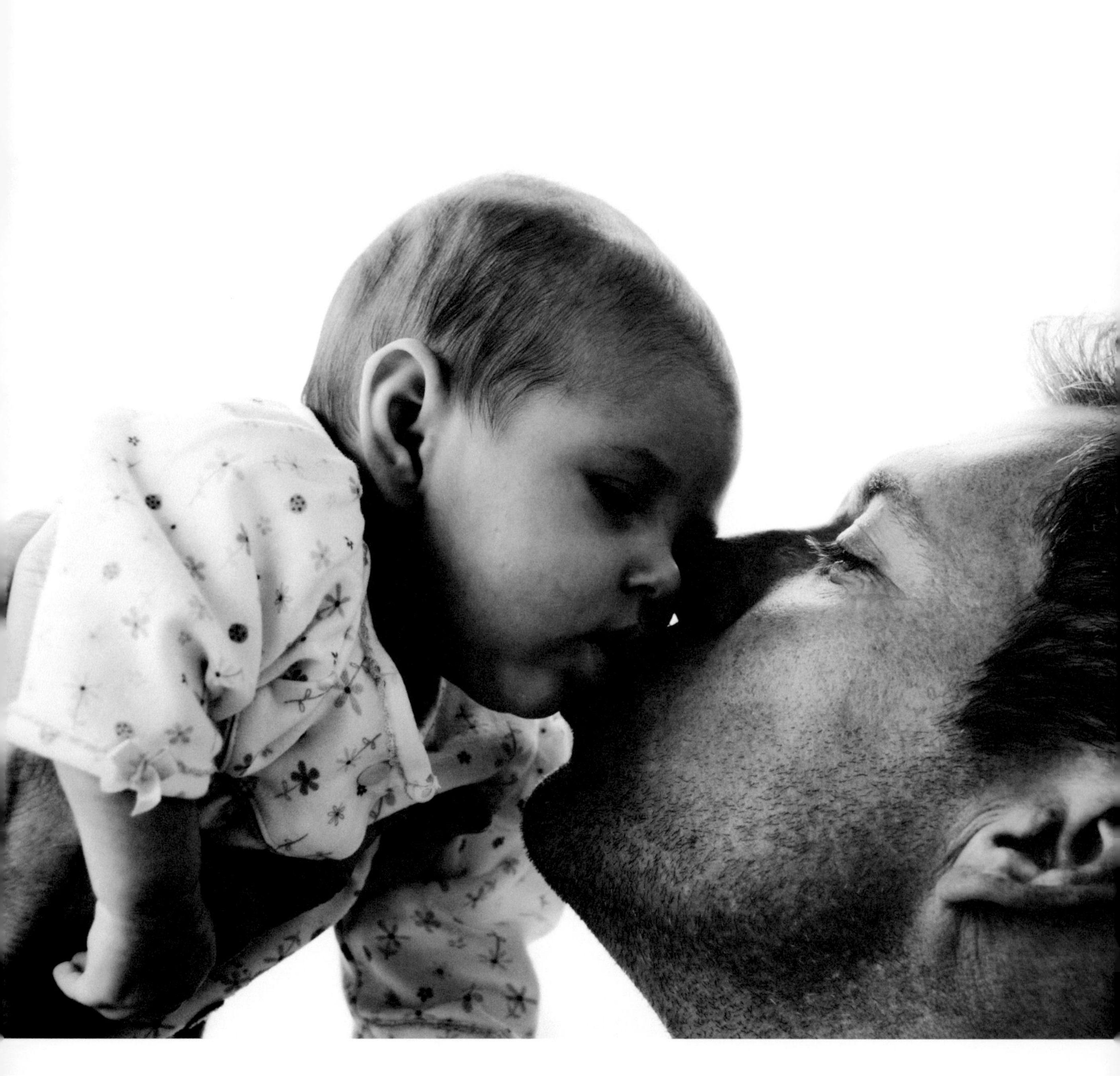

Twilight *Pas de Deux*

From my kitchen window
I watch my neighbor
join his two-year-old at sunset.
Their eyes meet and
the ballet begins.
He sweeps her up and
lifts her overhead
in fluid motion.
They twirl, they laugh.
He lowers her gently.
She leaps in one
direction, then another.
He follows closely,
but never overtakes her.
She extends her arms
toward him and he
dissolves into smiles.
Another lift, another spin
before they disappear
behind the door.

With each performance
I relive the pairings
with my own sons,
now grown.
I know how sweet the music,
how brief the dance.

~ *Ann Reisfeld Boutte*

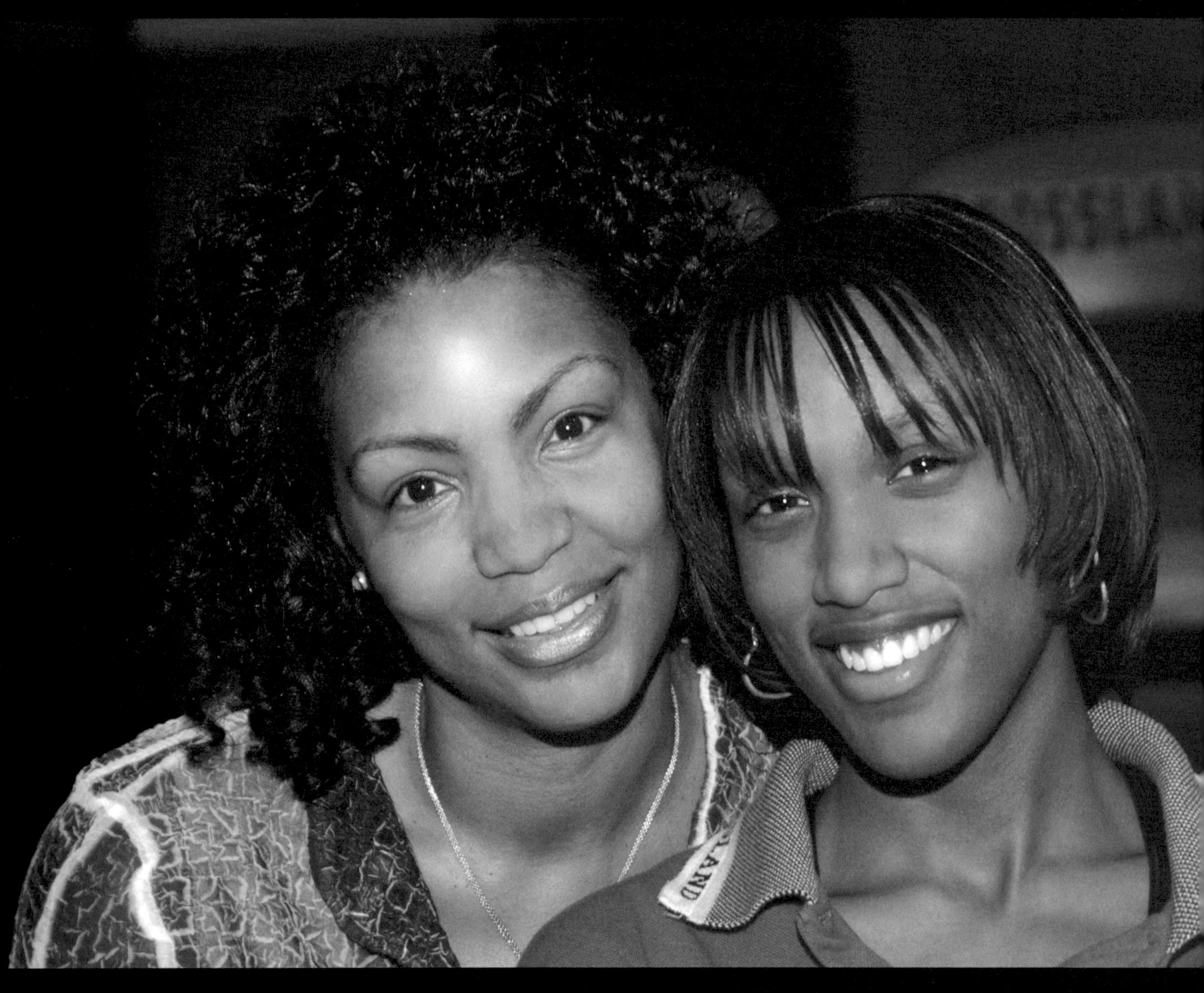

The Vine

A daughter is a vine that climbs her mother
like honeysuckle on an apple tree.
The mother grows toward light within this other–
the growing daughter–who, threatening to smother,
twining even as she's breaking free,
knows herself to be the vine that climbs the mother.

The daughter does not crush the mother, rather,
she takes up the slack reflexively,
as the mother grows toward light within the other,
reaching up, and doing so, discovers
that sky and air engender liberty.
The daughter, meanwhile, vine that climbs the mother,
uses all her limber tendrils, bending to uncover
the backbone needed for security
in a mother growing lighter in the other.

In time they will resemble one another,
although in season each blooms differently.
The daughter vine assumes the shape of mother.
The mother tree shines light within her other.

~ *Mary-Sherman Willis*

To My Daughter

What is there about the threshold?
There is no need to stand on it -
it is pleasant on both sides,
it is warm outside on a summer night
and you belong inside.

You linger on the grey stone step
two steps wide, an air lock
between hello and goodbye.
This is standing still
progression, and it takes hours.

I held your hand for many years
when we crossed the road.
Now you go out by yourself;
how long you wait on the doorstep
is entirely your own choice.

~ *Pamela Lewis*

Lost in America

I am the Geechee Girl. Lost in the English of America. Mangoes are what I like. Orange, green, and fleshy.

I prefer the heat, but when it's cold my grandfather talks to me from the walls of my house.

He says, "One day oona gwine see me agin. On dat day, we gwine rejoice fa true." Then I'm warm again.

My grandfather also tells me that I am the droplets of the Orishas, spilled into the womb of his wife. I carry the strength of my mamas, who were warriors, from Sierra Leone, Senegal and Angola.

Gather me mother and father. Gather me and give me the power to make my child the warrior she needs to be.

~ *Alicia Benjamin-Samuels*

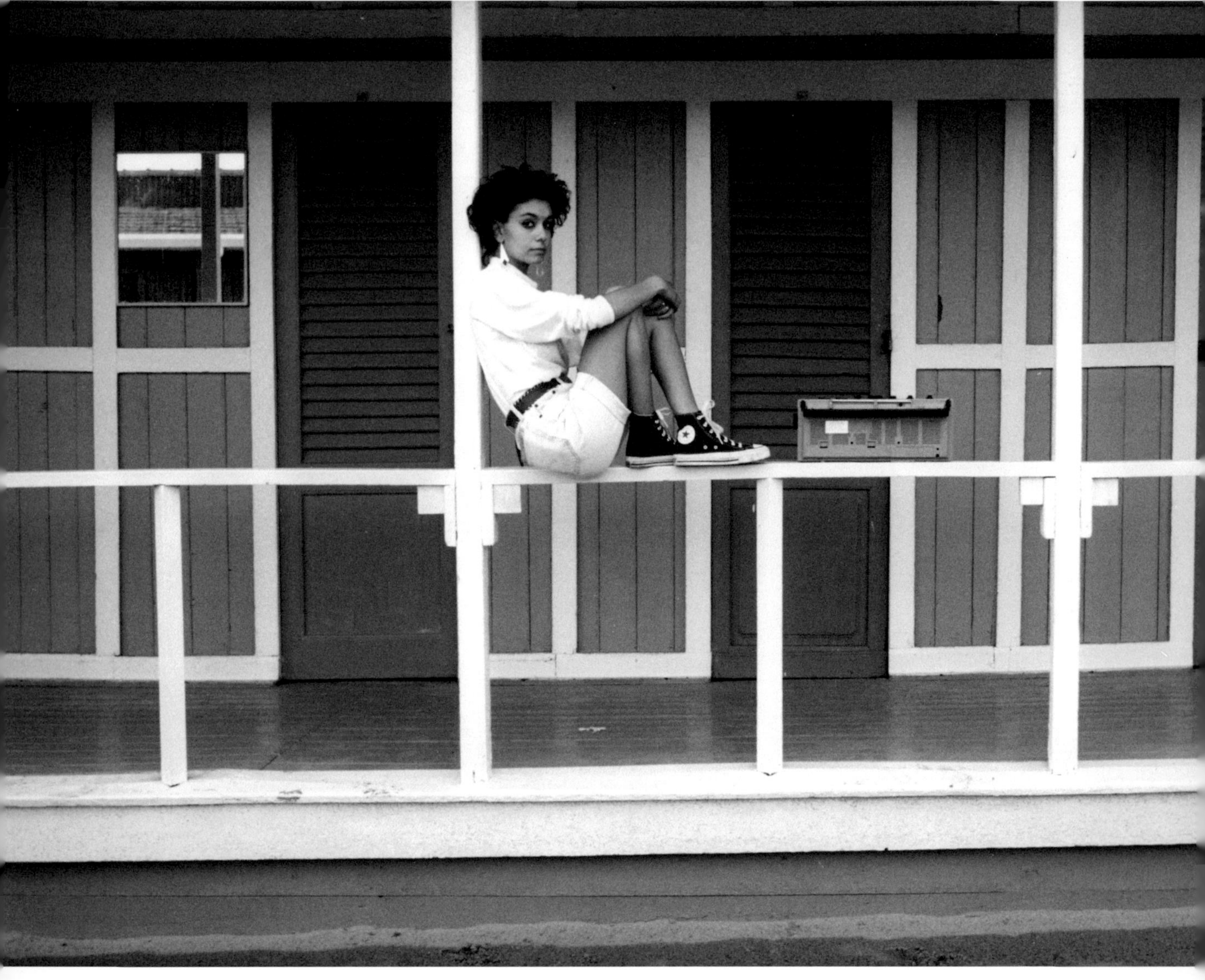

Rx: Poetic Therapy

To Ghana, My Teenager

Adolescence
Is a Disease
Unlike the flu
Characterized by the sneeze.

It strikes at fifteen
And doesn't care to retire
'Till the hair of the parent
Whitens or expires.

The brilliance of the age
Eludes high school tests,
Neatness and standard English
Take a back-seat rest

To Prince and the Revolution,
Tupac and Springsteen,
Red zits, green hair,
Adolescent screams.

You'll wake up one morning,
And all will be sane.
You can throw out your ear plugs
And smile again.

For this fade in/fade out
A parent's only instruction
Is to proceed with caution:
"Mature Person Under Construction."

~ *Sandra L. West*

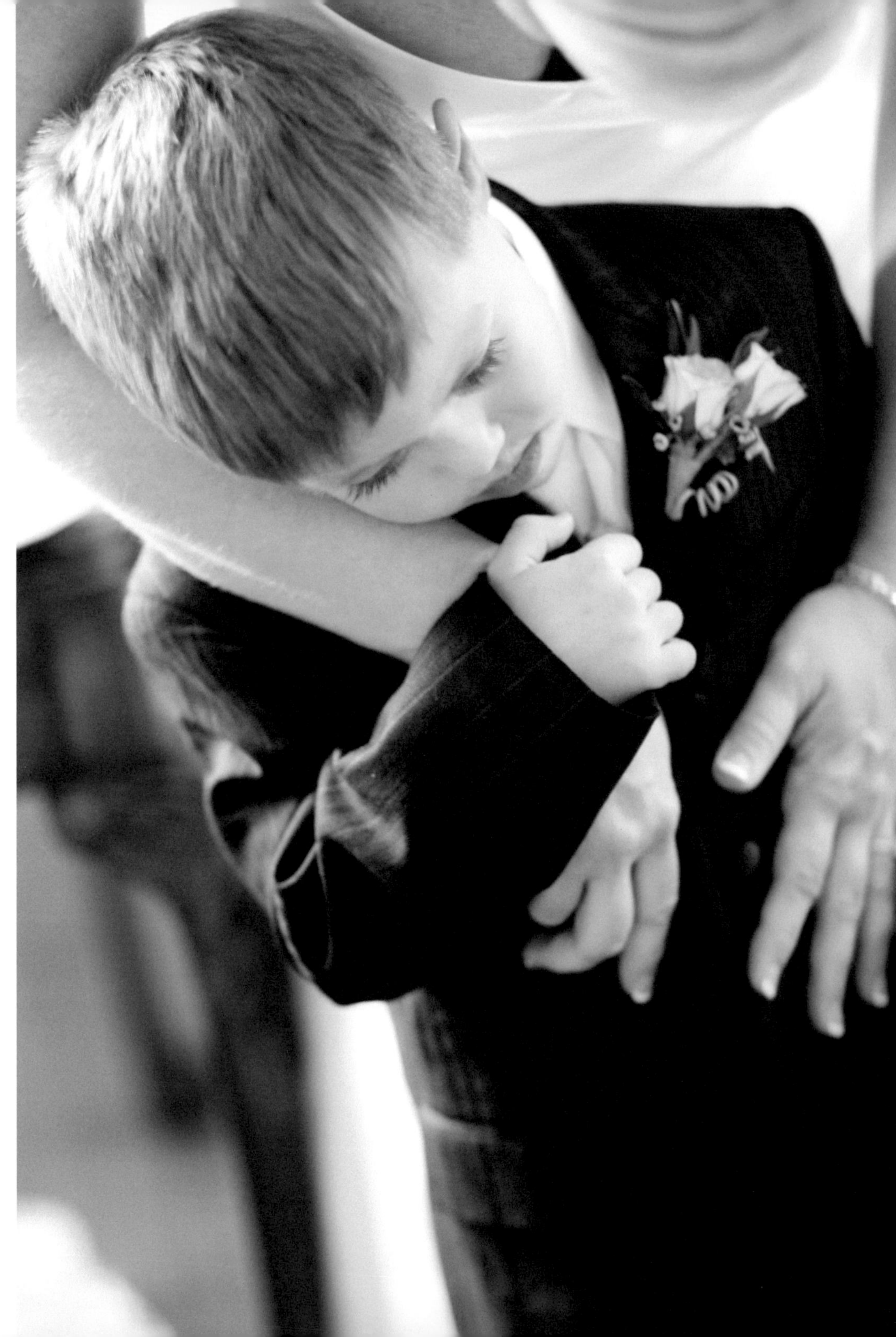

Mother and Son

I remember when he held my hand,
insisted on it,
though no longer a baby
or even a toddler.

Regret the times
I insisted he walk
unfettered by my fingers,

now that I miss those cheeks
that once fit into the palm of my small hand,
fail to see why I wished his high-pitched voice,
would break into deepening tones.

Was I preparing myself
for the cut ties,
the growth that leans away. . .

Am I nothing more than a loose string
unraveling at the slightest tug,
a wayward strand of hair
pushed back in annoyance
or without much thought?

I'm tempted to shake him back into my life
like a furious snow scene trapped in glass.
At the same time, want to close my eyes,
plug my ears, wish for ignorance,

ground him when flashes of myself–
ripples in the gene pool–wash over me
in a cold shudder like an October lake;
afraid history will repeat itself . . .

afraid he will swim in a sea of delusions
reaching shore too late,
waterlogged with regret
and blaming me
for the lateness of the hour.

~ *Lynn Tait*

A Parent's Revenge

After you have seized your freedom like the last piece of pizza,
declaring your independence with your mouth full of my food;

After you have ransacked the garage, the basement, and the attic
for every mismatched stick of furniture you can find;

Once I have shuffled my vertebrae, flattened a few fingers and a tire,
overheated my truck and my temper, helping you move into Your Own Place

a place you are proud of, responsible for, a place you actually have to pay
real money of your own making on time to a non-relative to live in;

decrepit couch here, brand-new stereo in the corner, the inevitable
duct-taped bean-bag chair, some posters, a braided rug with separation anxiety;

Just as you are kicking back in what was once my lounger,
with a cold drink and a self-satisfied sigh;

The doorbell will ring. It will be I—also known as me—,
come for just   a little   visit.

*

I may grunt a greeting or I may just walk right past you into the living room,
turn on the TV to a PBS documentary on Victorian wallpaper,
punch up the volume as far as it will go, stuff the remote under a couch cushion,
then leave the room to make a long-distance call on your phone
to an old friend on the other coast I haven't seen in years.

I'm going to stay up late, watching black and white movies
charged to your account, at which I'll laugh like a wounded warthog
each time you're about to drop off to sleep.

I'm going to borrow your car, borrow gas money for your car,
put a dent in your car and forget to mention it,
get a parking ticket and just throw it away,
break off the ignition key in the trunk,

then make sure to leave the radio on and volume cranked,
so you'll dump your morning coffee all over yourself.

I'm going to leave enough lights on for the space shuttle to land.
I'll make the hands on your electric meter
whirl like little airplane propellers.
I'll expect to eat out, every night, at your expense,
complain when we don't, but just pick at my food when we do.

I will rise each day promptly at the crack of noon,
then take a brisk half-hour shower,
drying each limb with a separate towel,
which I will thoughtfully leave on the floor
to sop up the water where I forgot to put the bath mat.

Then I'll thumb the thermostat to eighty
and open a few windows for fresh air,
letting the unsprayed cat out to play,
after I've fed her the tuna you had planned for lunch.

I'm going to use every utensil, pot and pan, dish and cup you own,
hiding some in each room, wedging the rest, unrinsed, in the sink.

I will gladly act as your personal answering service,
buying everything the telemarketers offer,
patiently reciting your credit card number to everyone who asks.

But I will do my own laundry: first, I'll yank out
everything you've left in the washer and pile it on the dryer.
Next, I'll take all you've left in the dryer and dump it on the couch.
Then I'll cram everything I've brought with me into the washer,
which will, when it hits the spin cycle,
dance the Meringue while its bearings melt.
I will dry each pair of jeans separately, for an hour.

All of this will just be my way of saying without saying
how much I miss you.

~ *Frederick Lord*

My Mother Ironed

My mother ironed in the flicker-light
of black & white, *As the World Turns.*
She sprinkled water on collars
from an old coke bottle to make steam.

The ironing board creaked rhythmic
as the iron glided graceful as a skater
over and over the white oxfords.

Mother wore shirt-waist dresses, no pearls,
never pants, looked like Donna Reed with no
makeup, scrubbed floors on hands & knees,
always careful to kneel on the red rubber pad
to protect her legs from further veining.

Mother made meals from scratch, boiled and mashed
potatoes in copper-bottomed Revereware. Kosher
chicken fell, obedient as children, off the bones,
to make the weekly Sabbath soup.

She hand-formed burgers in irregular ovals,
coated them in matzoh meal, fried them
in schmaltz and onions. The house
smelled always of garlic and grease.

I was eighteen before I had my first
McDonald's with my soon to be future
husband. My Mother disapproved
of both burger and boyfriend, wondered
how anything worthwhile could be
mass produced and purchased for fifteen cents.

~ *Sandra Cohen Margulius*

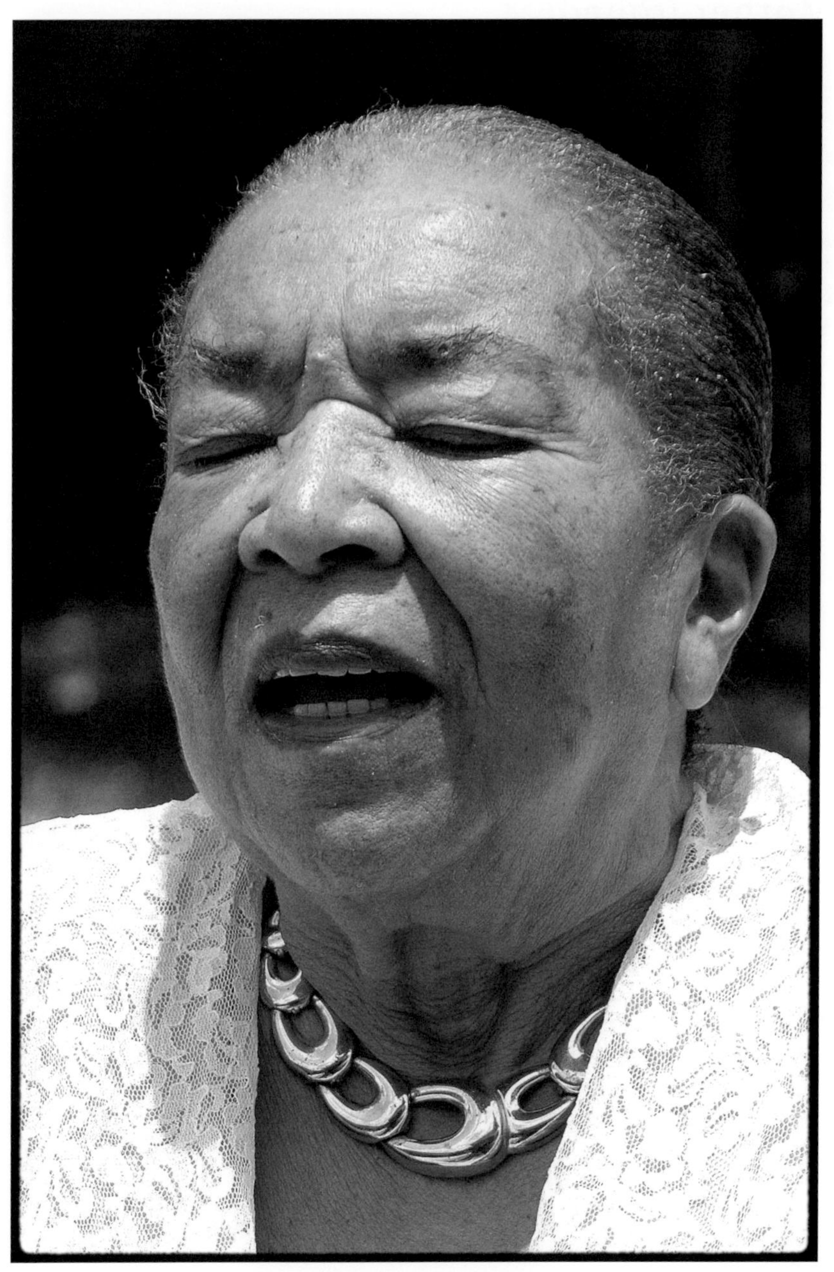

My Mother's Voice

rides the wind
finding me
even in the tall
grasses
where i lay
on my back
unraveling the stories
trapped in the clouds
firm like boiled green bananas
hers is not a voice
to be ignored
she insisted that things
were done her way
when i close
my eyes
her voice
is the waves at night
relentlessly subtle
a shimmer of indigo
not afraid of anyone
her voice quips
is who them talking to
even though
it was often tinged
with laughter her words
could be a hammer
nailing you to a cross
or the rustle
of the breeze
cooling you
on a hot day

~ *Opal Palmer Adisa*

Whistling Mother

My mother whistles under her breath,
all day, all the time. Not the sweet
song birds make but a toothy melody,
a skipped record, her lips pursed to a point.
She does this leaning over the sink
to peel potatoes, spooning coffee
into the basket, clearing the table.
She whistles in the car when she's not
sighing or sorting through tissues and bottles
full of pills. She does it while watching TV,
paging through magazines,
maybe even while she sleeps.
The tune is always the same, al dente
half song, a few notes rising and falling.
I wonder how my father can stand it.
Maybe he's just tuned her out,
after all those years of chucking nickels
into the jukebox of her mouth.
My own daughter tells me I do
the same thing, and I admit it, catch
myself sometimes–lips puckered, teeth
set, the air adjusting its wings, hoping the birds
are waiting, their ears cocked just so.

~ *Karla Huston*

Pastiche for a Daughter's Absence

It all comes down to what's physical,
this missing her—her face, voice, and skin.
I imagine my daughter dancing in Madrid, Barcelona,
and Seville, climbing the mountains of Andalusia.
I had not imagined how far away faraway would be.

Happiness, unhappiness—the same,
my sweet Zen master says,
and I wonder if the top of my head
supports heaven, or is this a migraine
coming on?

I circle back to the place where precision
and ecstasy meet, remember how I carried the tadpole
of her body, long before the first flutter, holding her
like a secret inside me.

I wake in the night missing
a body part, my arm stretched across the ocean,
hooked to the past, and I wonder,
as Achilles' mother must have,
Which part of you did I not dip in the water?

Heavy with absence, I hang curtains in her windows,
yards and yards of delicate Irish lace.
I hide behind the door, ear pressed to the wood,
and watch my daughter's life—her evening *paseo,*
late dinners in Saragossa's village square.
The room fills with the smell of *gazpacho, paella, sangria.*

Something like grief washes through me, something like joy.
I slip into the waves, feel the ebb and flow of her,
my water sprite, my sea nymph, remember the way
she glides through a room, the low-tide
of her voice, how she leaves us,
breathless, all fish at her feet.

~ *Diane Lockward*

Making a Salad

I find in this small task
the peace of what I have
and what I'll someday lose.
Tim Bowling, "Washing Dishes"

Such contentment, to stand at
the kitchen counter top, the lettuce,
bell peppers, tomatoes, zucchini
all laid on the altar before me, awaiting
transformation–the rinsing and peeling,
slicing or dicing, required of each
separate veggie that will metamorphose
the random green host into that oneness
that is a salad, the way a vegetable
both loses its self, yet becomes
a distinctive part of the whole,
as each child brings its uniqueness
to a classroom. Such pleasure
I find in this small task.

I didn't always feel this way.
Once, the making of a salad or any entree
was purely functional, a task to fill
a need. It wasn't until I was a father
I understood that food and who
prepares it and how is special and holy
in the eyes of a child. I grew
in the kitchen, donned apron,
not from sense of duty but
because doing it and doing it well revealed
the peace of what I have.

Our children now are parents themselves.
They shepherd around themselves
their own rites, their own ways to reveal
how important small things are in the life
of a healthy family. From the sidelines,
as I watch my sons assume their own
priestly kitchen roles I just smile
and reflect on all I've had
and what I'll someday lose.

~ *Glen Sorestad*

A Soul Returning

After Gerald Stern's Last Self Portrait

Now I know why Mama would look past me when I first arrived for a visit
and wouldn't help my efforts at small talk with her share of anecdotes;
and now I know why she smeared good health on her cheeks with rouge,
and would stick them out for me to kiss without feeling my touch;
and now I know why long moments without words hung
between us like hammocks filled with wet cement,
and she made a habit of gazing at some distant point–
like she was trying to see what lay ahead,
trying to glimpse the peace she wanted to be,
like she was trying to release whatever stood in the way
of her becoming that peace, including
her worn-out flesh.

~ *Carolyn C. Joyner*

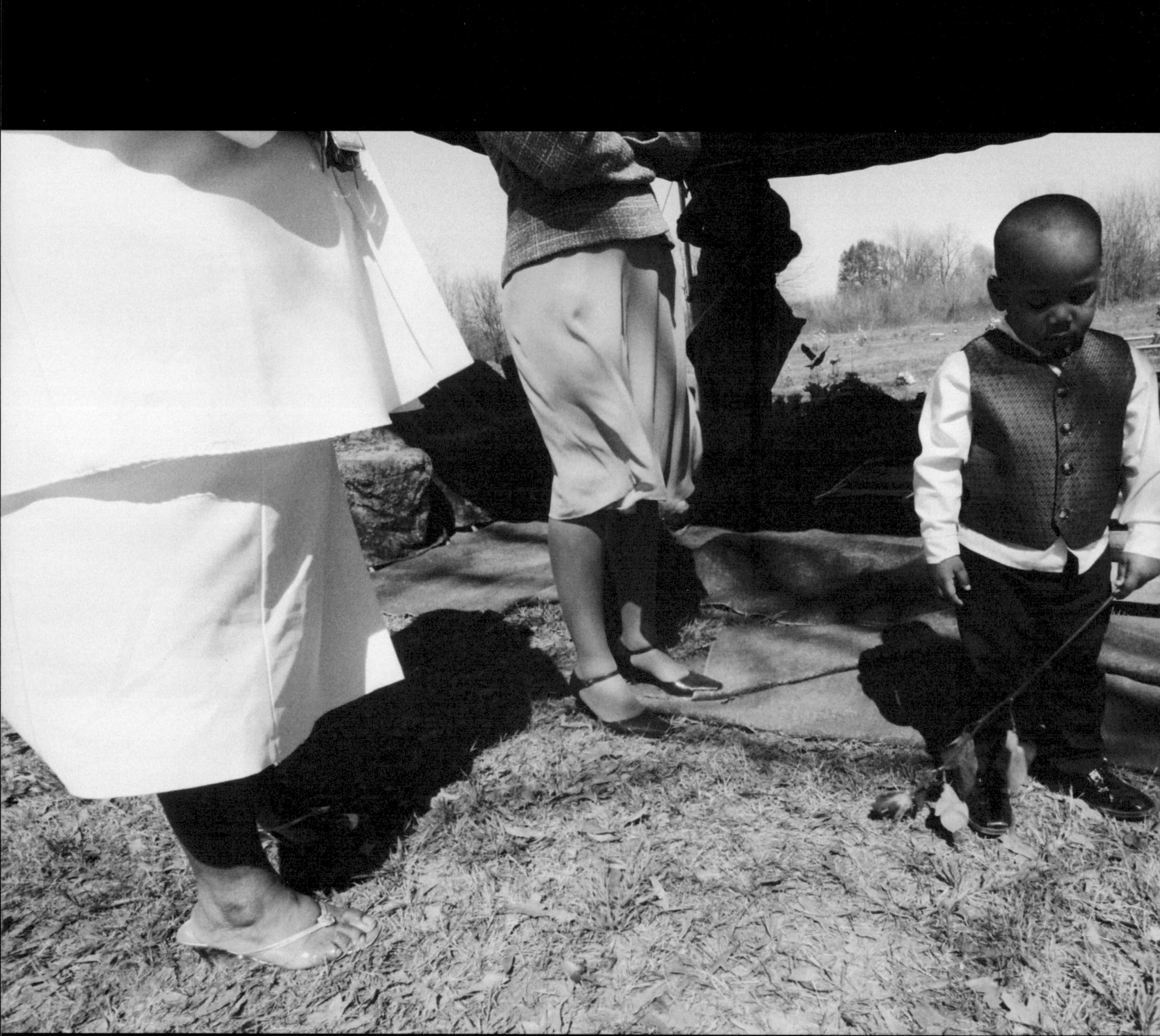

A Very Silent Man

How silent he was, my father.
I never remember him talking,
other than when he gave me instructions,
or reprimands about work.

How silent he was in prayer.
Every morning at first mass.
Every night before bed,
on his knees talking silently to his God.

How silent he was at work,
tending to his herd of mink,
like a sheep dog would tend his flock.

How silent he was at supper.
Eight voices clamoring, reaching, asking.
My mother filling plates like a short order cook,
begging him to "say something!"

How silent he was after lunch,
as he took his 30 minute nap
before returning to his mink,
his chores and his silence.

How silent he was with his rosary
woven between his fingers,
wearing his blue suit as we stood
wordless around his coffin.

~ *Charles P. Ries*

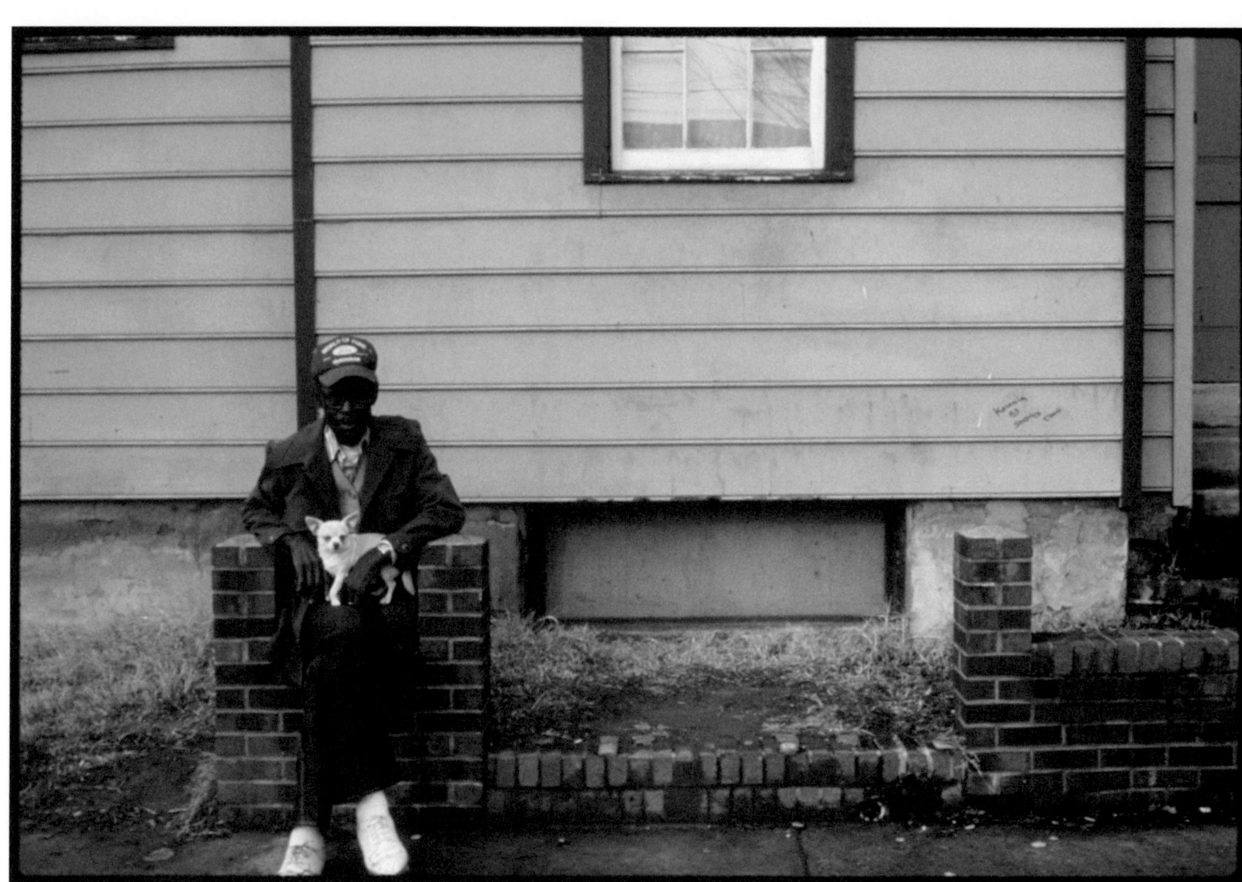

History

(4 my grandpappy Henry who died 11/15/94 and left me here)

You asked if we were close.

i visited him once a year;
more if i could.
He gave me three things i loved:
watermelon, sweet potatoes,
and sense of who i am.
He told me i look like my mother;
called me little Janie Ruth–
that is not my name.
He smelled like tobacco
when he hugged me.
"I love ya girl," he said.
He couldn't read, but i wrote him letters.

You asked if he was a good man.

He called regularly to tell us his ass was cold;
we took him two pairs of long johns each year
along with a cap to cover his balding head.
When he was sick,
he never forgot who i was.

You asked what he did.

He drank-
a lot;
he wore caps i gave him cocked to one side;
he worked the land he owned
hard.
The last time i saw him
he was not lying in a blue and silver box.

He was sitting
in his rocking chair
on the front porch of his house
on land he owned
in Rabbit Bay
on Temperance Hill.
Smiling, he told me he was proud of me.
He does not know:
what i do;
where i live;
or what i have become.
He knows:
i am his ;
he is mine; and
HE WAS LOVED.

~ *Askhari*

When I write poems...

I picture Grandma in her old wooden rocking chair
Her life an oracle's tale
Her black womanhood bringing enlightenment to the west
Parting my lips like hair
To grease my tongue with wisdom
Arthritis hands gnarled like tree
Fingers the fruit of passion for her people
When riding in her '96 green Toyota Camry we were on the Serengeti
Our safari car navigating our displacement
She like a queen mother of Ghana and I a sphinx
She came from a long line of conditioned little black girls that at some time or another grow old
In my eyes she saw progression, change, and power
Peeking through bifocals is a hardened soul
With spirits spanning from New York to the continent
Now she sits in nursing home
With a matrix of rooms
Every day choosing between the red and blue pill
Swallowing pride down with them
When I write poems
It is her and the ancestors whispering in my ear

~ *Alison C. Rollins*

The Gift

After the accident, the hospital
they brought me aching home
mouth pumped up like a tyre
black stitches tracking the wound
over my lip, the red slit signalling
the broken place. And my son
my tall, cool son of sixteen
kissed the top of my head
and over the curve of my shoulder
laid his arm, like the broad wing
of a mother bird guarding its young.

Anyone who has known tenderness
thrown like a lifeline into the heart of pain
anyone who has known pain bleed into tenderness
knows how the power of the two combine.
And if I am a fool to give thanks
for pain as well as tenderness
and even if, as some would say
there are no accidents -

Still, I am grateful for the gift.

~ *Chrissy Banks*

I Go Back in Time and Rescue my Mother

I know just where to find her, standing at the stove,
frying potato latkes in a cast-iron skillet. Her apron
is spattered with dark spots of grease, and waves
of heat rise up from the stove, pasting her dark hair
against the dampness of her neck and temples.

"Can't you make them any faster?" I am asking,
ten years old, at the table with my brother and sister.
The little pancakes are made of raw potato, grated
into a bowl and mixed with egg and salt and pepper.

It is dark outside, early winter. I arrive as a gust
of cold air, blowing in under the front door, hovering
in the space over the table, over the serving plate
with its bed of paper towels to absorb the excess oil.

There have been so many times that she's said,
"I just want to run away," spoken in anger
and in desperation, that I expect her to come
willingly, to take the ghostly fingers I offer
and allow herself to be pulled away

from all of us, from that life–the whining,
bickering children, the unfulfilled ambitions,
the husband who works long hours and listens
from a distance. The loneliness. The emptiness.

Everything that I know now she must have felt.
"I can save you," I whisper, pulling at her hand,
but she slips away, turning instead toward the table,
squandering what feels like her only chance for escape,

though the door is unlocked and she's chosen a million
times to stay. So I seep out of my childhood
home and go back to my own life. To the whining,
bickering children, the unfulfilled ambitions,
the husband who works long hours and listens

from a distance. The loneliness. The emptiness.
My mother calls on weekends after going
to bookstores or concerts, after sleeping until ten.
I stand at the stove, cooking hot foods over cast iron.

When my daughter arrives from her future life
to save us both, I find that I scarcely feel the hint
of air on my hand. But I am ready. I've been waiting
years now for someone to come and rescue me.

She pulls my arm away from the clothes I am folding,
from the dirty dishes and the trash that needs to go out.
And we get all the way to the front door before I hear
her voice–nine and a half years old, siren sweet rising
up the stairs–and find that I, too, am unable to leave.

~ *Leah Browning*

Perfume, and Silence

Kalahari Desert, Southern Africa

My mother visited me one night.
She sat on my bed, like she used to
when I was twelve, and touched
my forehead with featherlike fingers.
Why aren't you home? she asked me,
her voice hollow as wind.
She had been dead nine years.

But I had no words to answer,
no words to ask how she had found
me here, in Africa, or where
she thought "home" was. Her body
was air. Even the odors of whiskey
and decay, present always on her,
were only faint perfumes.

It was the dry season, and still.
Night birds passed my open window.
I would not speak to the dead.

So she faded then, after a while,
slowly, to dim sparkles suspended
in the dusty silence. She vanished.
I didn't forgive her.

And outside, the moon turned black
in the sky.

~ *Christopher Conlin*

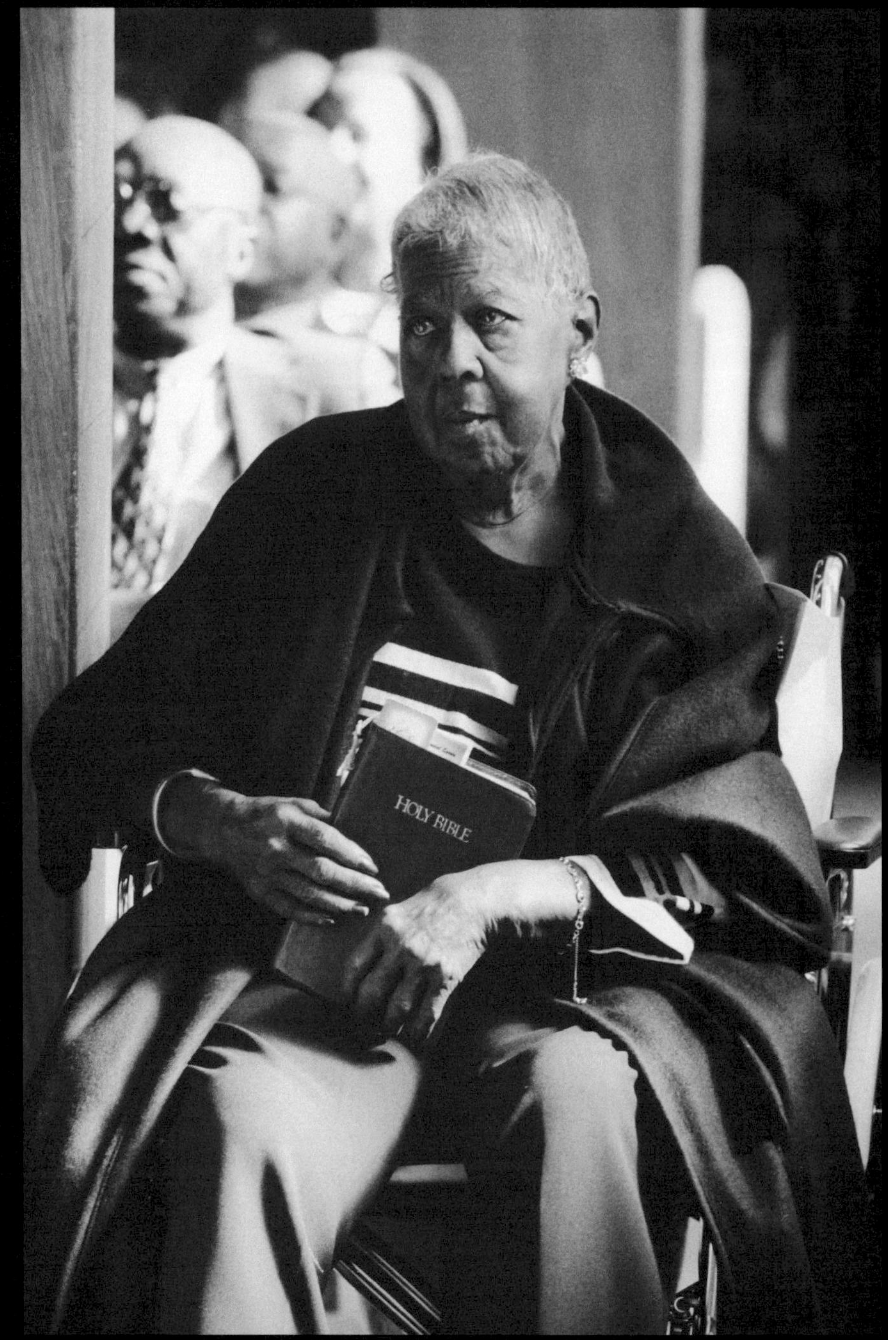
HOLY BIBLE

My Grandmother

How do you tell
the Matriarch to
lay down
take away the keys
remove her 85 pounds
from the land
she hustled for
saved and twisted
the system to purchase
her shit
for her kids
she'd never say it
that way
but those noses she wiped
now save her from
incontinence

How do you demand
or convince
the Matriarch
the Africa
the hymn
the endless work woman
it's time to sit
for rest she might get
she can understand
stopping between other's loads
and the awaiting of her own
laundry as the sun creeps into
the horizon
but this sit has no end
it does not travel
it must wear Depends
not ready to die but can
not live alone
the crumbling castle can't

be lived in
no other breath inside
Paw Paw died in 2005
makes it not a home
cats prey like vultures when
she's all alone

I combed and braided her thinned hair
my last time home,
saw her for the first time
her muscularly frail naked body
did it make her feel dethroned?

How do you move
the Matriarch
from her sweet silent throne
without mocking her legacy
before she is gone?

~ *Natasha Ria El-Scari*

Inheritance

My mother wonders aloud why I stare at the photo
in the tarnished frame. It is her mother,

who died when she was ten. I question my mother
daily. She tells me what she can remember:

That her mother sat in a rocker by the window
drinking black coffee when it snowed. That she

loved purple. I file secondhand memories, buy lavender
curtains, cut milk and sugar from my coffee. In her portrait

she sits, serene, dark, her hair a thick halo. She wears
a floor-length frock, gloves, buttoned boots.

Alone and widowed she raised three daughters and
three sons in a south filled with trees and torment.

And I think how I fear for my son, the traps set for him
in twenty-first century America. I want to live

for a moment in memory, sit with her by the window,
sip from her favorite cup. Let Grandmother be

our salvation. Take a picture in sepia.
Show the future who we are.

~ *Matilda W. Cox*

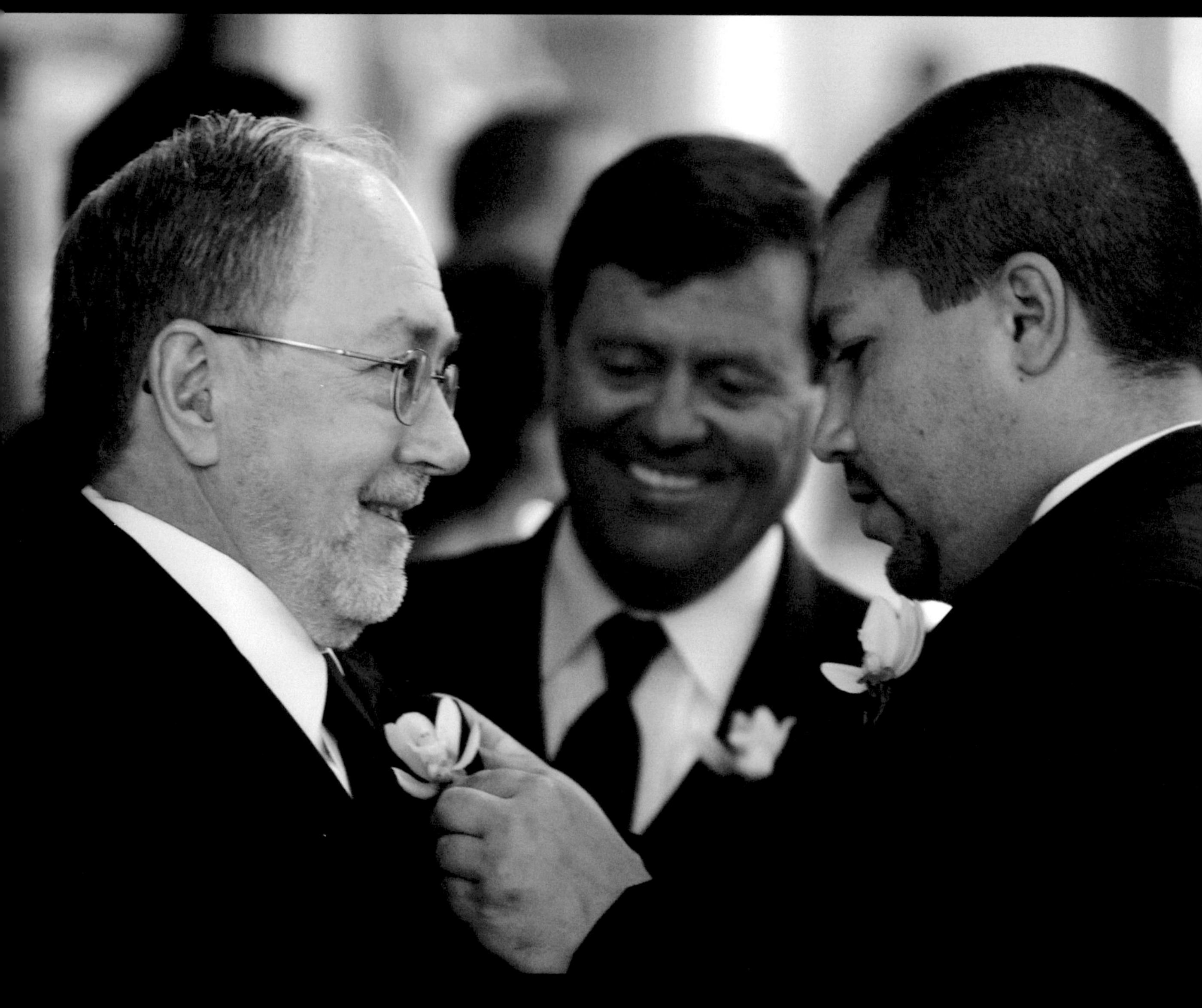

My Eyes

At 27
On my father
In the mirror
Standing behind me
Tying my tie...

Funny to be learning this ritual now,
Getting the trick of it, how the longer end
Wraps double, loops through an opening
The shorter end tightens.

He has this down pretty well,
Though not much of a tie man himself,
Only on special occasions, only in the way
An extremely unspoken bond pulls at us,
The knot holding while not being a noose.

Father, despite years of many small strung-
Together words, despite times unavailable
& privacy gestures freeze, there's certainly
A larger time, a given, no photo has ever cramped

For we weren't snatching at closeness then.
It lived on its own with the knowledge
We could not possibly fail
In our strange love territory.

It is this knot my eyes find in this mirror
Tying us in the trusted distance
Locked finger firm

~ *Stephen Mead*

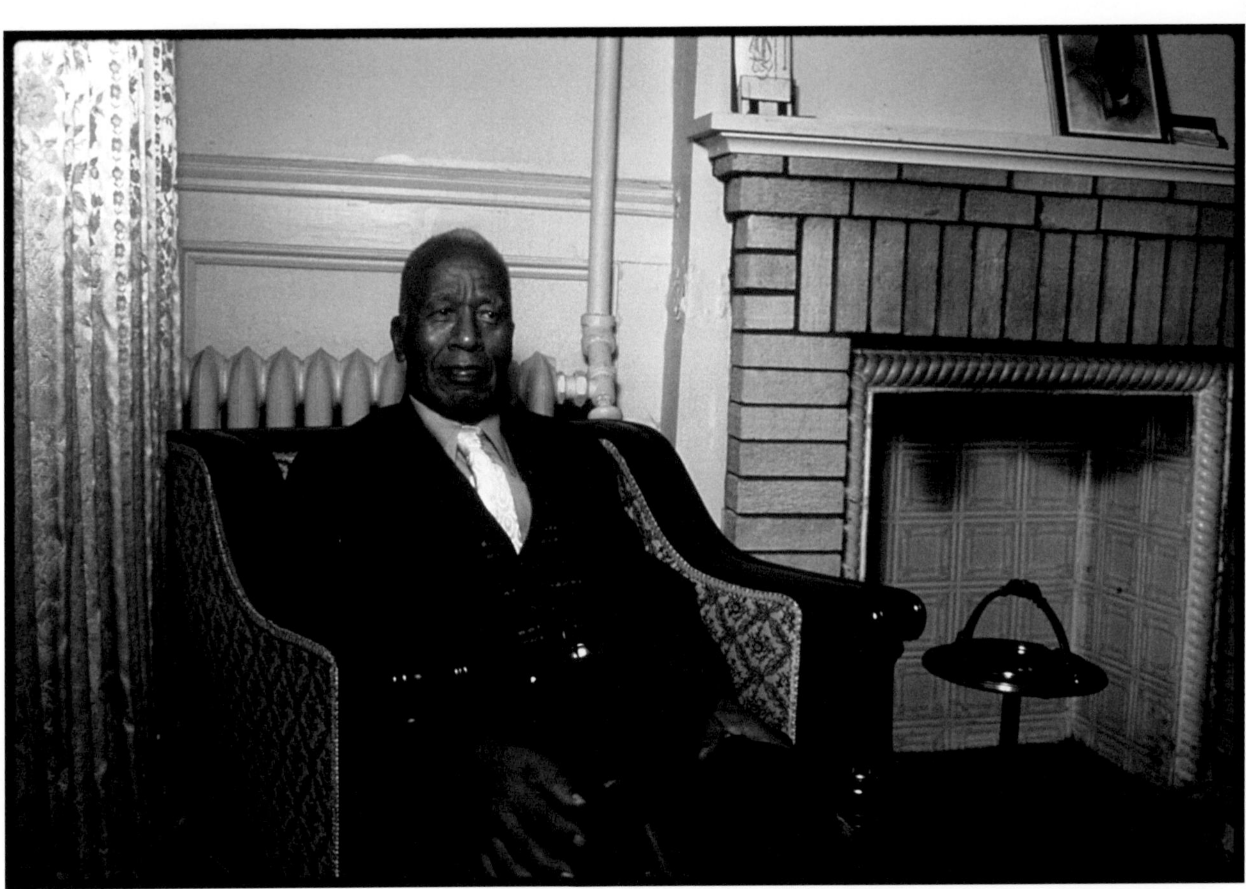

Alzheimer's 2/9/06

my stepfather doesn't remember me
my face has lost
all magnetism
i am a woman
young enough to be his daughter
but old enough to be
somebody's mother he's quite sure of it
we converse about places i have never been
in years i have never existed
i remind him of his wife
my mother Patricia Ann
the way i walk flailing both arms
prodding through air
with an inexcusable desire to be freed
from the last stride
you the spitting image of Ann
he says the way she moves
she always in a hurry
like her nerves ain't settled
or the ground is on the fire
burning through her shoes
you must be her sister
he reminds me that soon he'll marry Ann
and move to natchez
some place wide with neglected space
where she can pacify her nerves
while he coaxes betsy his mule into bringing in the feed
he says one day
you'll visit us
with our children
sipping homemade lemonade
watching the sunset through sugarcane stalks

you just wait
you'll see
yeah you Ann's sister
i figured you right
you got a lot of Ann
round the eyes

~ *Mawiyah Bomani*

The Final Shenanigan

The seven of us in our same seats
at the fake-marble Formica table,
the mashed potatoes and the meat loaf
with the baked ketchup a crimson streak
down the middle, and yawning ahead of us the inexplicable

math homework. Then someone might say Daddy,
Daddy, please, please do that trick.
No, not tonight, I'm much too tired. Amazingly,
we'd believe him, always taken in by his malarkey.
But minutes later his baby blue eyes rolled

into their black sockets, the hand under his chin
gave way, his wide mouth went slack.
Immediately, all five children would begin
laughing uncontrollably, some of us certain
we'd wet our pants. Not tonight, Charlie,

our mother would say in that stern tone of voice.
But it had begun. Slowly, in what was only a few
minutes, but seemed like it lasted half the day–
one by one his arms and his legs gave way
until finally, he had contrived

to slowly, oh so slowly, fall off his chair,
and onto the floor, sprawled on the waxed linoleum
like a dead bear. In excruciating
quiet, no one brave enough to touch him,
we waited for his eyes to open, for this pratfall

to end, his hands to move. Now, I kneel here, dare
to stroke his hand which is inhumanly cold and dry.
The morticians have given him the wrong smile, a spare
thin-lipped affair; his cheeks are roughed like a girl's.
Daddy, what was that game we played and why

did we play it, thrillingly anticipating
your unmoving limbs, your silence, your collapse?
Were you preparing us for this morning's
final shenanigan when you don't climb back up
onto your chair, and we all go home for dinner without you?

~ *Kathleen Sullivan*

Lessons

I could have died
in that curious square
smooth and cool in the basement
a brother on the outside counting by two's
a child's breath on the inside
behind the old refrigerators door
hide and seek folded for fun
he ran away to escape my screams
his silence was a fist beating
against the door I could not open
curled back to fetal
wrapped in the dark like before
I waited to be delivered birth or death
can look the same
before the light comes
with arms spread and relief
in my mother's face

~ *Ijeoma Thomas*

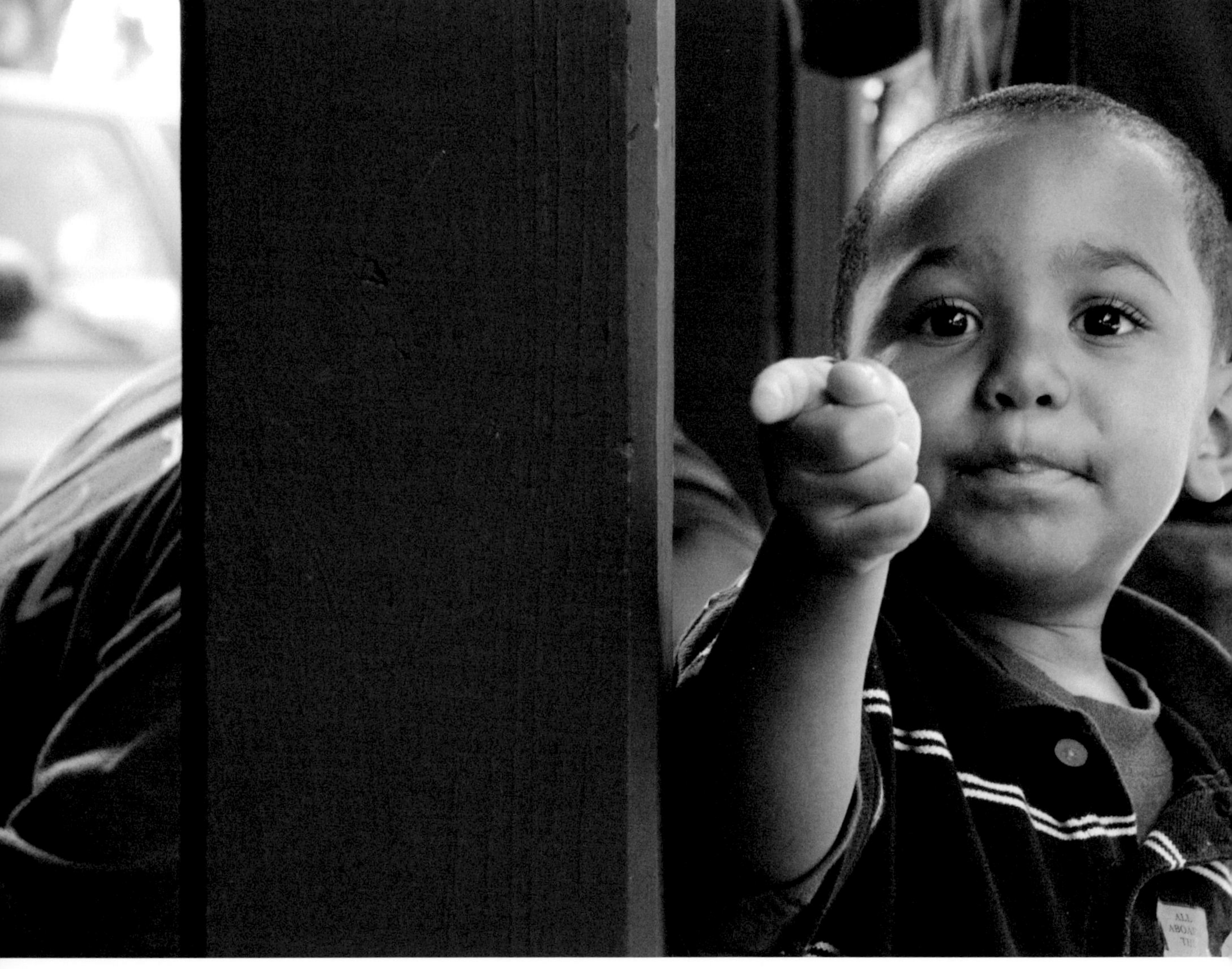

Who???

Who spilt what on the rug?
Leaving that ghastly stain, ugh.
"Not me, not me, not me!"
Who let the toilet overflow?
"Don't look at me. I don't know.
It certainly wasn't me!"
Who ate the Oreos? The crackers?
Categorically all deny they're snackers.
"Not me, not me, not me!"
My angelic children all agree
With enviable serenity,
Whatever the calamity,
"It wasn't me!"
And what I want to know
Is where did the culprit go?

~ *Phylis Warady*

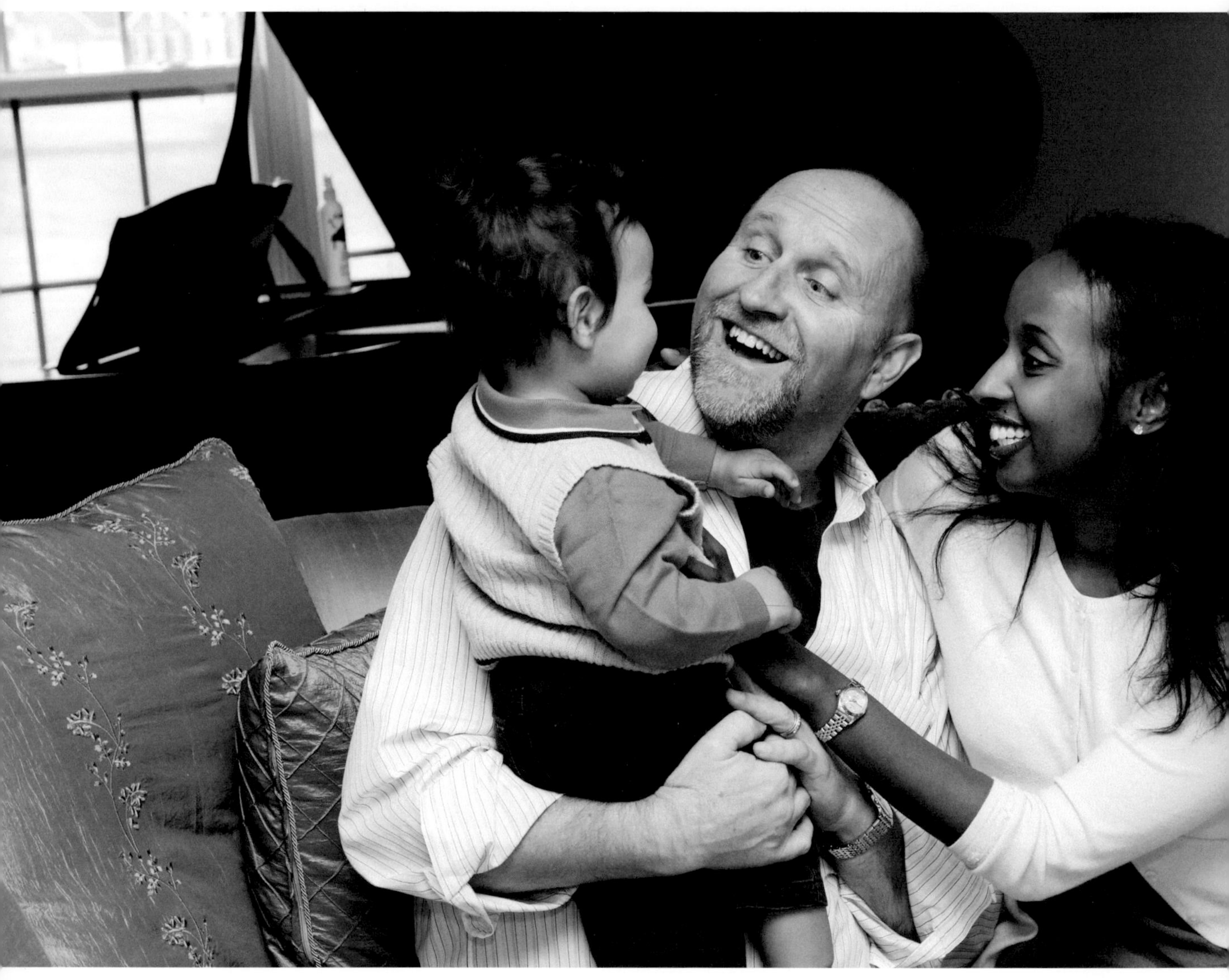

Home Sweet Home

Like old shoes on bare feet
Like soft blankets on cozy beds
Like good food to eat
Home Sweet Home
Like laughter with a best friend
Like sweet hugs from a loving mother
Like summer days that never end
Home Sweet Home
Mom's smile
Dad's laugh
Grandma's Cakes
Grandpa's Love
It's great to be home
Home Sweet Home

~ *Monique Brown (age 9)*

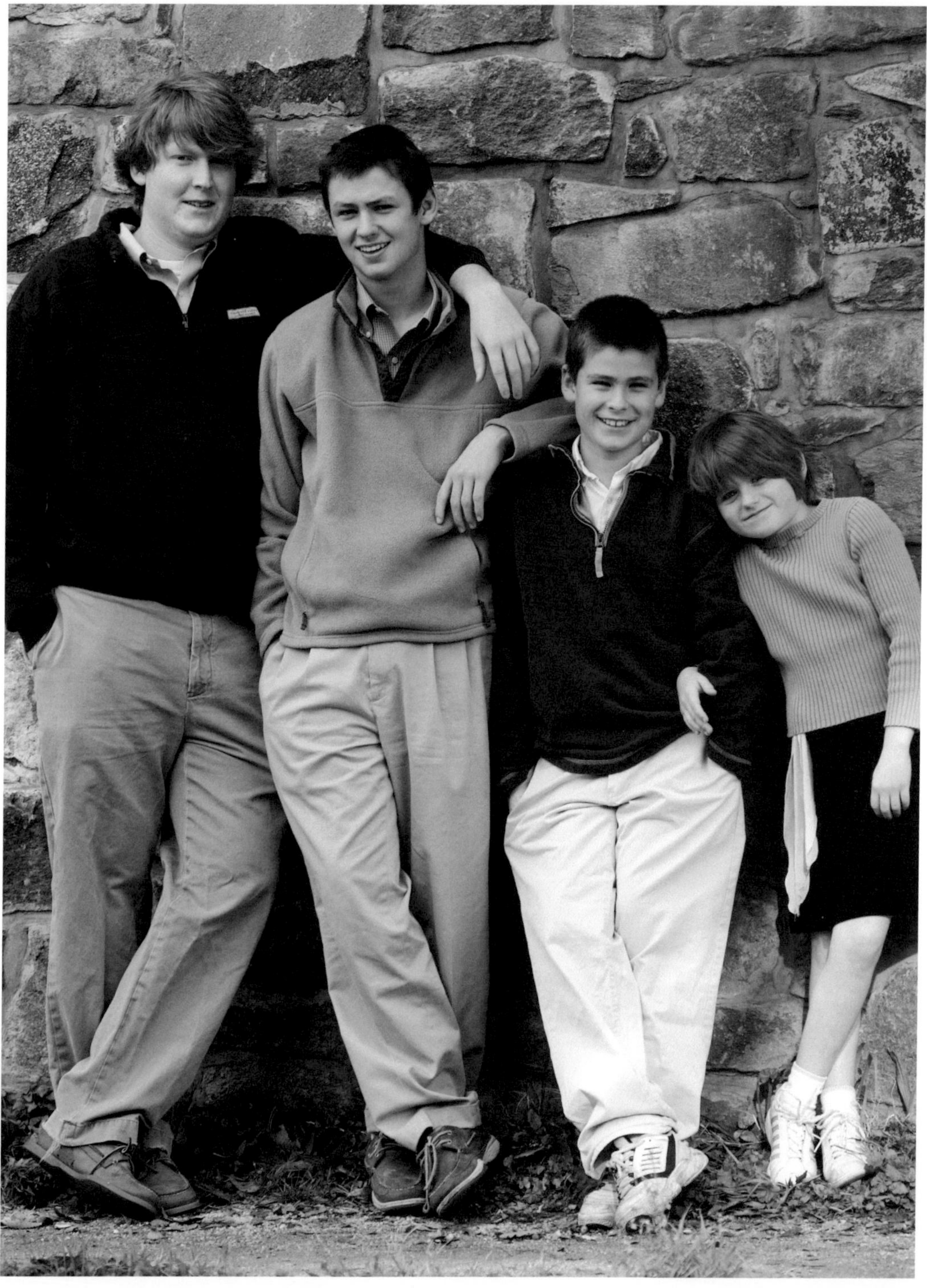

Tall Sons

You tower over me,
now six-foot-five and six-foot-three,
with broad shoulders, quick minds,
capable hands –
grown men, knowing so much more than I
about so many things.

But I still ache to hold you
in the shelter of my arms,
still long to smooth your path
so you won't stumble,
light you way
so you won't stray,
and know that you are safely home each night
before the dark grows dangerous.

~ *Joy Harold Helsing*

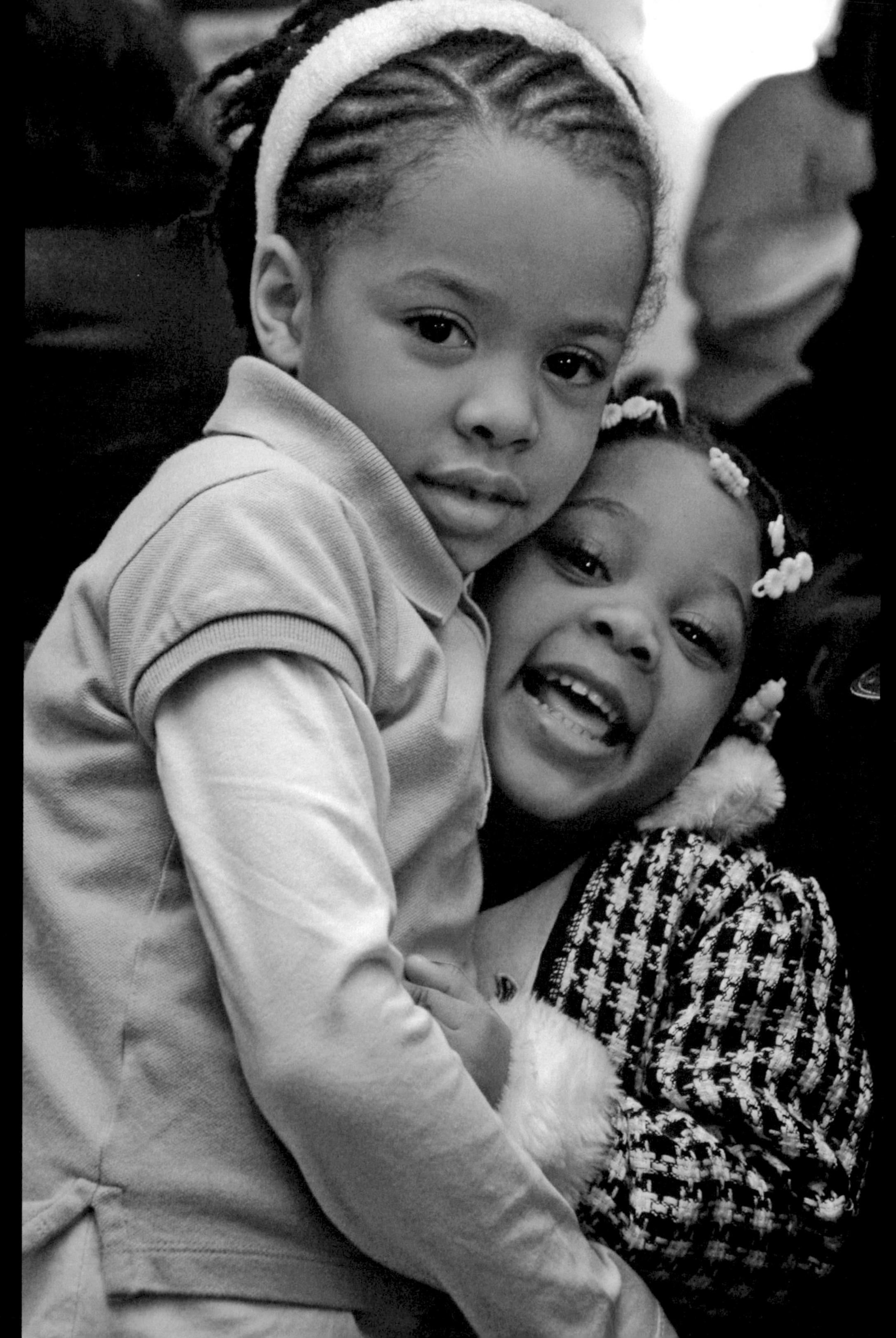

A Poem for Little Black Girls

For Kadi

If ever sweet reason to live forever more
Encourage positive influence for
little Black girls to soar.
Inspired by thirst of twinkle in bright eyes
Inquisitive intelligent innocent years
    race by.
Our precious lovely little Black girls
Oh so dear to our happy hearts
Awake with morning dew
prepare for new challenges right choices
    each fancy fresh start.
Instill goodness of love in character while
    willing, eager and ready to listen.
Rewards of hard steady work in future shall
    perpetually glisten.
Sensational power of prayer
Bountiful blessings and graces hasten
    toward all our little Black girls.

~ *Sylvia Dianne Beverly*

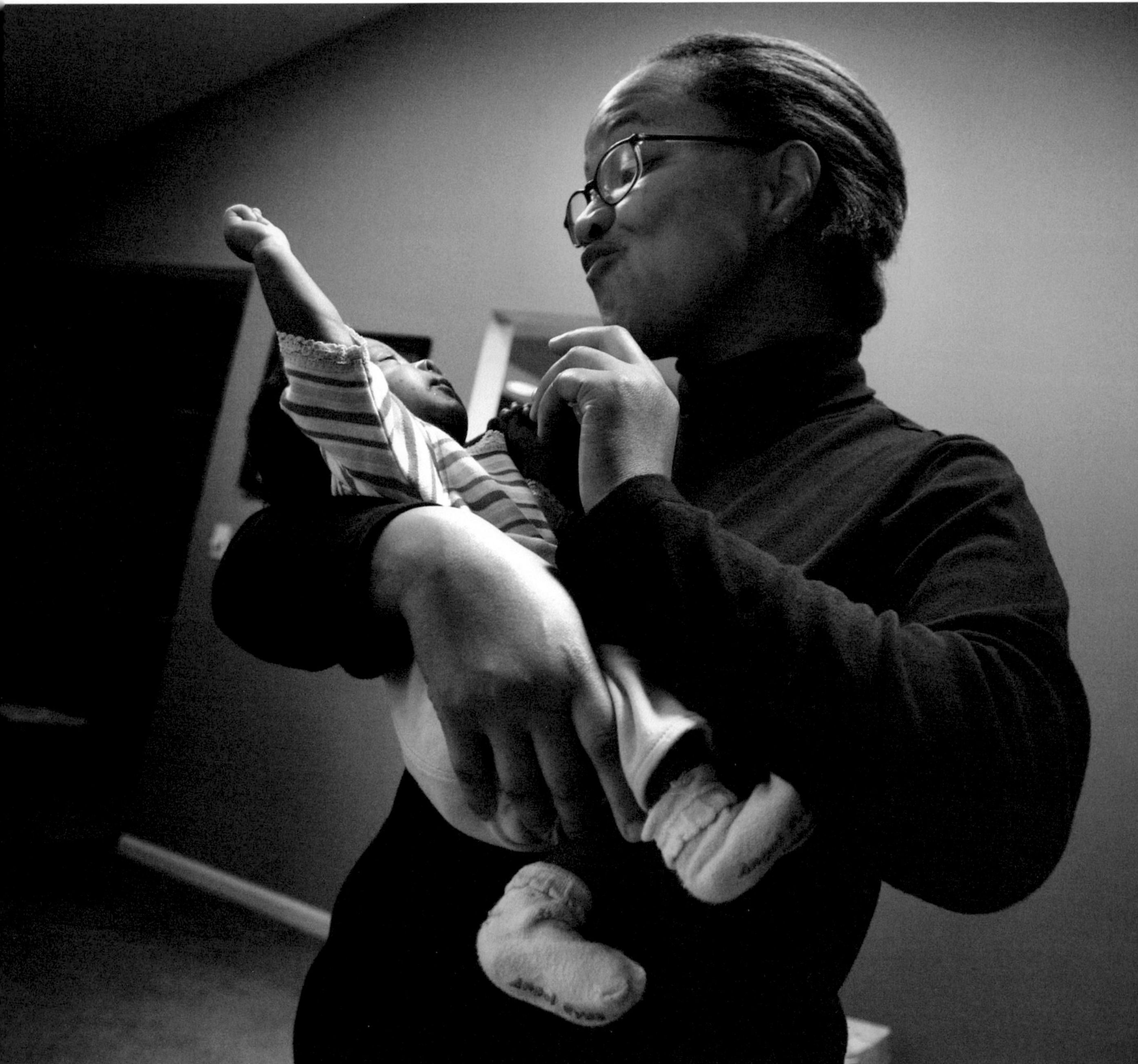

the klan marches washington

my mother walked the mall
her bell-bottomed corduroys
swirled against yellow gravel
no stroller
she held me close,
curled me in one arm
like a swan
the other swayed her side
determined

on the lawn,
men simmered
under cotton cloth,
hailed and hawed
and stomped their boots to the earth
tried to crack freedom to its center
like a summer shell

my mother, with her platform shoes
filled to the buckles,
tip-toed behind a brown line
of people with hopeful signs
swaying in song
we shall overcome

shielded by lullaby
she swung me into both hands,
my body squirming in the air
and lifted me up over her head
as if to say

oh yea?
segregate this.

~ *Katy Richey*

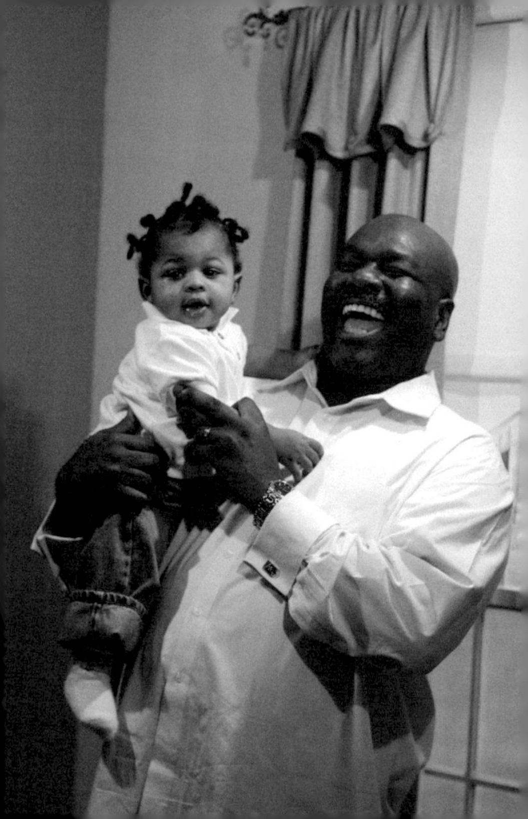

Little Brown Baby

LITTLE brown baby wif spa'klin' eyes,
    Come to yo' pappy an' set on his knee.
What you been doin', suh–makin' san' pies?
    Look at dat bib–You's ez du'ty ez me.
Look at dat mouf–dat's merlasses, I bet;
    Come hyeah, Maria, an' wipe off his han's.
Bees gwine to ketch you an' eat you up yit,
    Bein' so sticky an' sweet–goodness lan's!

Little brown baby wif spa'klin' eyes
    Who's pappy's darlin' an' who's pappy's chile?
Who is it all de day nevah once tries
    Fu' to be cross, er once loses dat smile?
Whah did you git dem teef? My, you's a scamp!
    Whah did dat dimple come f'om in yo' chin?
Pappy do' know you–I b'lieves you's a tramp;
    Mammy, dis hyeah's some ol' straggler got in!

Let's th'ow him outen de do' in de san',
    We do' want stragglers a-layin' 'roun' hyeah;
Let's gin him 'way to de big buggah-man;
    I know he's hidin' erroun' hyeah right neah.
Buggah-man, buggah-man, come in de do',
    Hyeah's a bad boy you kin have fu' to eat.
Mammy an' pappy do' want him no mo',
    Swaller him down f'om his haid to his feet!

Dah, now, I t'ought dat you'd hug me up close.
    Go back, ol' buggah, you sha'n't have dis boy.
He ain't no tramp, ner no straggler, of co'se;
    He's pappy's pa'dner an' playmate an' joy.
Come to you' pallet now–go to you' res';
    Wisht you could allus know ease an' cleah skies;
Wisht you could stay jes' a chile on my breas'–
    Little brown baby wif spa'klin' eyes!

~ *Paul Laurence Dunbar*

Dad Haiku

Love is like Heaven
giving everything of self
a priceless treasure

~ *Regena "Sonray" Reighns*

Grandpa Jack

Grandpa Jack was a big man.
He would sit at his big oak desk
with a big stack of papers, surrounded
by big certificates in big frames
reading big books filled with
big knowledge. He was a big man.

Sometimes, the grandchildren would
seek small answers to big questions.
Grandpa Jack would lean back in
his big black chair. He would pat
his big belly filled with fried chicken
and penny candy, roll his big eyes back
in his big head to find the knowledge.
And for hours, the children sat and
sighed, in his bigness.

Grandpa Jack used a lot of big words.
He spoke of freedom and education,
of oppression and liberation, of choices
and dedication. Of love. His lessons
from the past were designed
to secure my future. He told me
I had big responsibilities ahead.

Then, one day, Grandpa Jack fought
the big fight with the Big "C". and lost.
His big belly swelled and fell. His big
laugh faded. His big speeches slurred.
His big heart stopped.
His big spirit moved on.

But Grandpa Jack's legacy lives on
as I seek big answers to small questions.
As I write of freedom, education
oppression, liberation, choices and
dedication. As I write of love. I sigh
and remember how big a man
Grandpa Jack really was.

~ *Michelle J. Pinkard*

Monsoon Reunion Before the Tsunami

for A after the Peace Corps

Forty-eight hours by plane, train, and tuk-tuk
to reach the last lap—a leaking long-tail
boat that sputtered between rocks, squalls
and swells. It coughed us onto sand where
dark hands of island gypsies pulled our salt-
crusted limbs from the Andaman Sea.

The body told the tale of transit. Swollen feet,
muscles taut from lines and lugging, the ache
of locked bowels and trapped intestines.
Lungs expelled stale air and squalor;
a heart pounded loose from tight moorings.
More than a year of waiting. Calls crackling,

the sudden flood of the familiar trailing off
into night silence. Flimsy blue letters,
blurred photographs, hunting for the scent
of a daughter's life. Then, the path led up
from the foaming sea, up white limestone cliffs
to coconut palms, a school, a hut cut into the jungle.

Yellow beaks, red-striped wings darted
between the green. Light and heat swallowed
the air. `Continue 28 days after exposure.
Avoid sun,' read the doxycyline bottle.
Glasses steamed, a hat wilted in the island's
glitter and glare. Shaky legs carried me up.

Higher, a shadow loomed. Ridiculous,
I whispered, warding off gibbons, rats,
elephants, untying the thread of blue letters
fingered like worry beads through long seasons.
White tinged clouds rolled in from the sea.
I pushed my glasses high on my head,

focused on the shape growing taller, tanner
than memory. A sudden breeze freed
a figure from the web of dreams.
She was running, trailing orchids and lotus
blossoms. Jumping and laughing, we banged
into each other. Bones and flesh melded.

Crushed petals sweetened our scents.
Claps of thunder, falling drops. High
above the sea, we were wet cheeks
and sheets of water, a mother and daughter
wrapped in the damp cocoon of each other
and the monsoon just beginning.

That was Koh Phi Phi then, when there was
only rain, only a monsoon. Then before the loss
of families, homes, children, the island itself
sucked under the sea. Now there is only
memory–memory of an island, a day,
a daughter safe in my arms, her life just unfolding.

~ *Davi Walders*

search and recovery

for James Kim (1971–2006)

it could have
happened to any
of us

a wrong turn
down a logging road
tires tunneled
into snow

a man's undying
love for his children

moves satellites
maps aerial images

18 care packages
dropped over 16
miles of the Siskiyou,

bearing handwritten
notes from a father
to his son

the signs
you left for those
who came after you

a red t-shirt
a wool sock,
a child's blue skirt

layers of a life,
stripped down to
a family's fate –

the weight of being
unseen–to travel
a path back to

what you knew
at birth, the warmth
of being held close

brought home

~ *Shin Yu Pai*

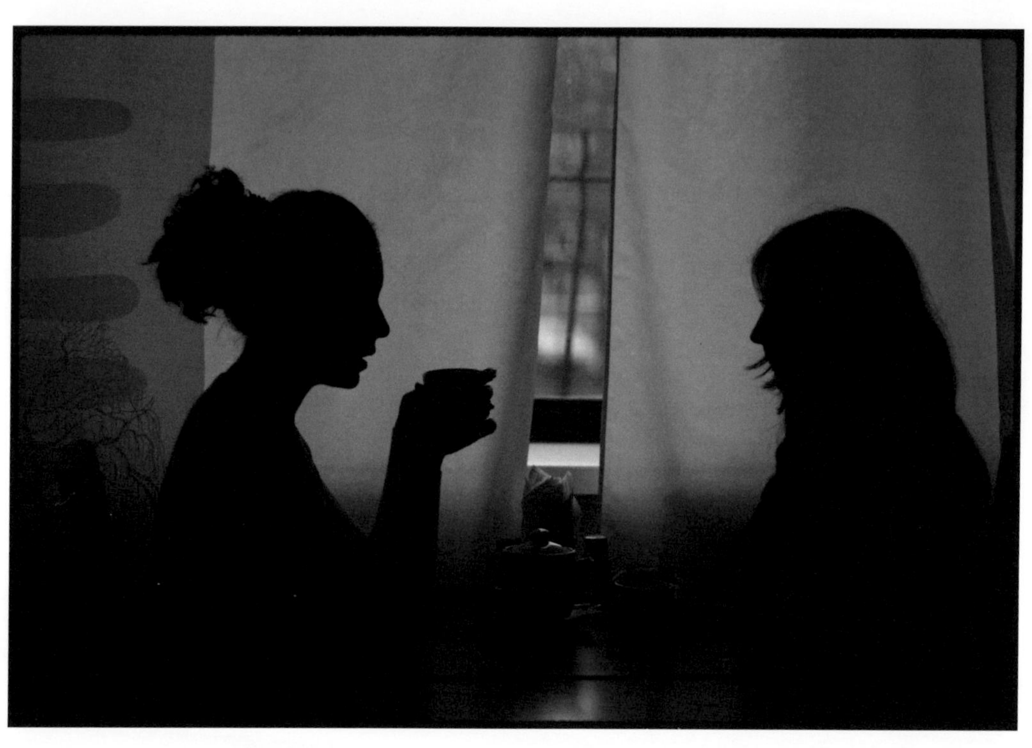

Reading Tea Leaves

Drain the fragrant liquid, drink
in the scent of jasmine –
my mother taught me this –
tip the cup, translucent as time, fragile
    on its impossibly thin rim, drops
    the color of old blood seeping
    onto the saucer beneath:
three quick turns clockwise
    to set the past
    to approach the future –
her mother taught her this –
    lift the cup and peer into its open mouth
    to see what it has to say.

My mother explained to me nothing
of the dark shapes' meanings:
    how a lock means obstacles ahead,
    how a mask is a secret that must be kept,
    how scattered beads of a broken necklace
        show danger ahead in love,
    how an army of ants signal a host
            of impending difficulties.

We sat together on winter evenings,
my mother and I, in a cool ring of light
illuminating Formica and chrome,
imagining brown-stained blossoms as hope,
picturing houses–the signs of comfort–
under trees, which signal health,
our fast friends as dogs, and
stems and sticks that became the figures
of those who would surely come to visit
if we made out their initials nearby.

No time for boiling, stirring, straining–my tea is in bags now:
every house of comfort washed away
the dogs long dead and buried.
The lip of cup is mute, escaped flecks choking the open throat
(gathering ants or scattered beads, what does it matter?).
dipped and drained, the leaves sulk in silence
within their shroud of mesh with its tether of string
wherein all the letters of the alphabet are drawn.

~ *Christina Lovin*

Carolina Beach 1967

I open my eyes and the windshield
of our 59 New Yorker is a deep blue green.
I shove brother's head from my shoulder
and aim it toward little sister
curled up in the corner
of the back seat.

Mother hugs a beach towel and props her head
against an armrest as her bare feet
dangle out the driver's door.
Dad's sunk deep in a beach chair snoring
with an empty beer can perfectly
balanced upon his exposed belly.

I dig for the remaining Fritos
from the bottom of a rolled up bag
stuck between the seats and take a warm sip
of Sprite from a can on the dashboard
before I crawl out the back window
and run for the water.

As I stand on the edge of the ocean
in the early August morning
I do not know that in less than a year
my mother will refuse to answer the door
when the men in uniform appear on our front porch
to deliver the news of my oldest brother.

I do not know that twenty-two years of marriage
can be dissolved by mixing sadness
and alcohol or that death separates
those closest as often as it unites
leaving emotions scattered
like eggs on an Easter Sunday lawn.

I do not know that the inability to embrace
the inevitable will result in pugnacious showdowns
no one can win while faith
is pondered daily and fingers pointed
in all directions as even the most
sacred taboos are shoved into the open.

I do not know that mother will run into the night
with a strange man on the eve of my eighth grade year
and become a voice on the phone
for the rest of her life or that father
will dive deeper into a bottle he knows well
offering no excuse for the fall.

I do not know that at the age of forty
I will be the last of four brothers breathing
as I attempt to understand a world
I can't control by putting words on a blank page
in hope of defeating the demons who play
musical chairs inside my head.

All I do know is that we have five days
reserved at the Surf-Side cottages
on BEAUTIFUL CAROLINA BEACH
and I should wake everyone
so we don't miss a minute
of the time we have left.

~ *Jason Kelly Richards*

My Father Speaks

After he had been dead eight years, I couldn't remember
the sound of his voice, the tenor, the pitch, the Iowa inflection.
Maybe I never knew what he sounded like,

all of the years he was living, but moving away from me,
becoming memory before his body died. There is always
one price for forgetting, another for remembering;

the sound of his voice rides on the back of a memory
of his face, his hands large, fingers clicking together like sticks;
the dead, unrestful, unbury themselves

when we think too long on them, our thoughts
like a thin rope down into the earth, their pale hands
pulling up and up into an unaccustomed light.

A voice just now, through the window well;
a voice from the back yard, a voice from the trees.
It reminds me of someone. I cannot see who is speaking.

~ *William Reichard*

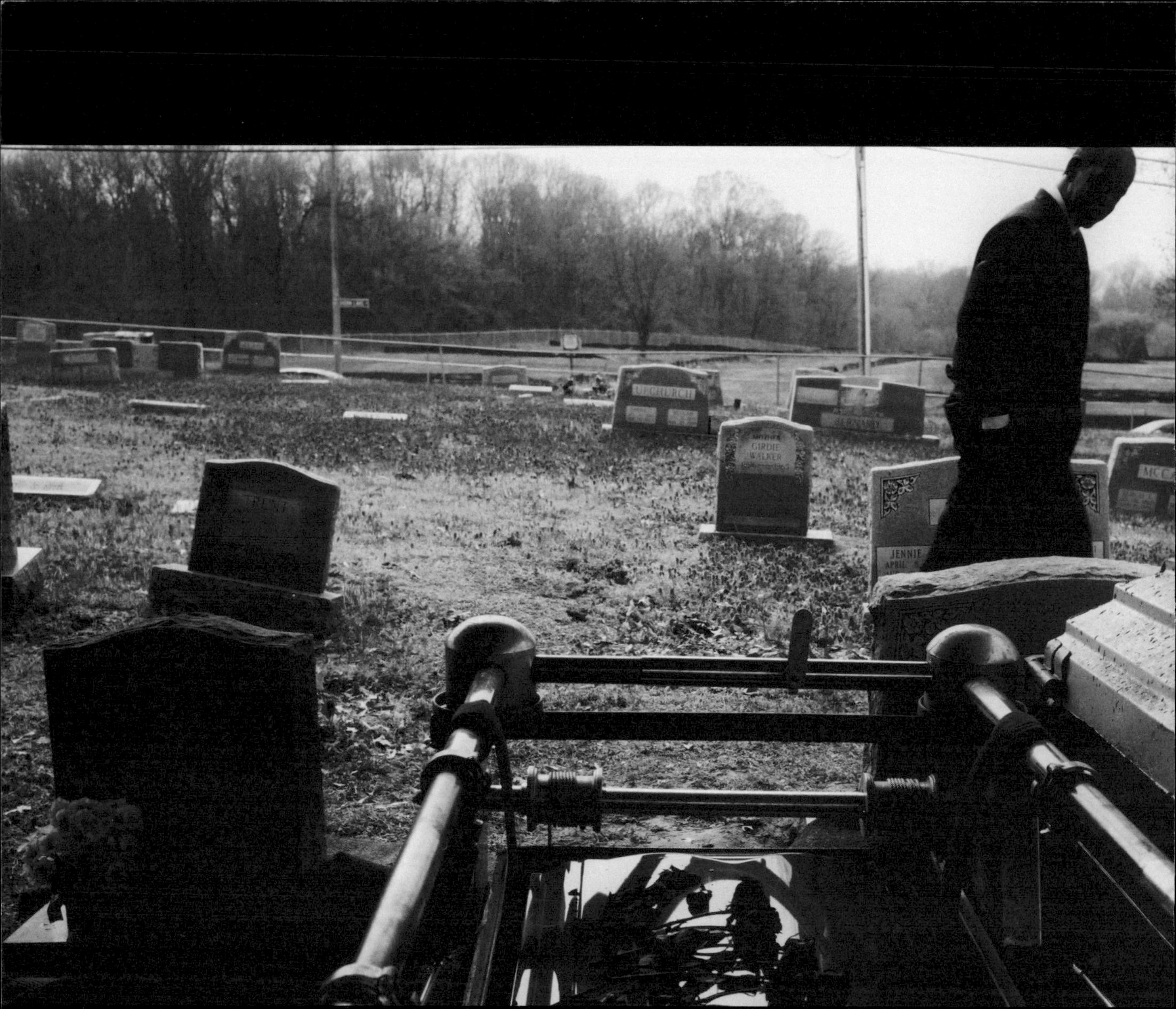
GIRDIE
WALKER
JENNIE

Did you enjoy your funeral?

(For Ruth Smith Daniel: Sunrise 1908 - Sunset 1999)

how did it feel to be back
on a saturday morning?

in your old church?
in your old deaconess uniform?

old christians testifying how close to god you were

your favorite pastor
preaching from your favorite scripture:
            the 23rd of psalm

your family sitting in front of church
for a change

did you enjoy your funeral?

            i didn't.

you deserved a crucifixion turn-out

that church should have been congested with devout tithe givers
not some loose congregation of grieving family
wearing easter clothes from two decades ago

you were a christian
who believed in people

who gave religiously
and made sacrifices for a living

maybe i was agitated by your pastor recruiting sinners in-between hymns
looking at me in my african garb
like an empty collection plate

10 years ago
i was feeling jesus and this church
now my beliefs have changed
like my name

sitting on the same pew that i used to sleep on
makes me nostalgic
about Sunday night communion,
waiting for the "claiborne"
by the "magnolia" project.
no one at the bus stop
but an elderly woman and her great grandson

no one was going our way
so members left us hanging
like those suits i used to wear...

II

i've been a seasoned pallbearer since the age of 13

when my mama introduced me to death
you inherited a teenage son

i have no mothers to bury anymore

my altar is full
like the 91 years you were here

i forgot how to cry on cue
so tears come unexpected

like deaths in our family

life without you is a lot to carry

that's why no coffin
has been as heavy as yours

~ *Nadir Lasana Bomani*

My Father's Auden

My father's father used tiny pins
to force his son to learn the Koran.
For every mispronounced word, forgotten phrase, too tangible a pause–
a mark was made.
My father's hand would erupt with blazing stars,
his fingers veined like oranges.
When his palms filled with blood,
Grandma would press them with lilies
until both skins were pink and dripping.

On my sixth birthday I received a leather bound copy of The Odyssey,
pages gleaming like the domes of ancient temples,
the far-away land of my father's home brought to me,
in my, not my father's, native tongue.
"This, Angelique," he said, "is the first of many threads.
I give it to you without consequence."

In his books my childhood splayed open like a pomegranate.
Shakespeare, Dante, Dickinson spilled across the floor
where toys might have been left. Once, he caught me
awake in the fold where night leans into dawn,
Auden frozen in the trickle of moonlight.
My father took the book clutched in my hands,
replaced it with his fists.

Inside them,
inverted Braille
arced from thumb to pinky.
"This," he said,
"is what my father gave to me."
I ran my fingers across the markings–
trying to read their meaning.

Only after reciting a passage
from Auden to a college lit. theory class
do I realize:
I do this to fill the holes in my father's hands.

~ *Carly Sachs*

After Virginia Tech

My father calls to make
sure I'm ok, his voice
an awkward
star in the constellation of dark
miles between us. In our
patchwork family, he is the
one kneeling in the corner,
examining these strips
which used to hold
together, as if tight knots would
never come undone. He
an observer while my mother
opened herself for the feeding.
My father the immigrant
wants me to take caution
in a country where he has learned
how to be lonely.
Out of his mouth swims a name from the Asian
American textbook of my past –
Vincent Chin.
Do you know the man mistaken,
beaten to death?
Yes, I say.
But these are stark lessons he has never
taught me –
his own jobs not won,
which dreams he has left.
We never speak of these things.
Tonight,
he is singing a lament
for those families without second chances,
for men who sit in the darkness
with no one living in their hearts,
for a country he once believed could be
his own,
before all this.

~ *Ching-In Chen*

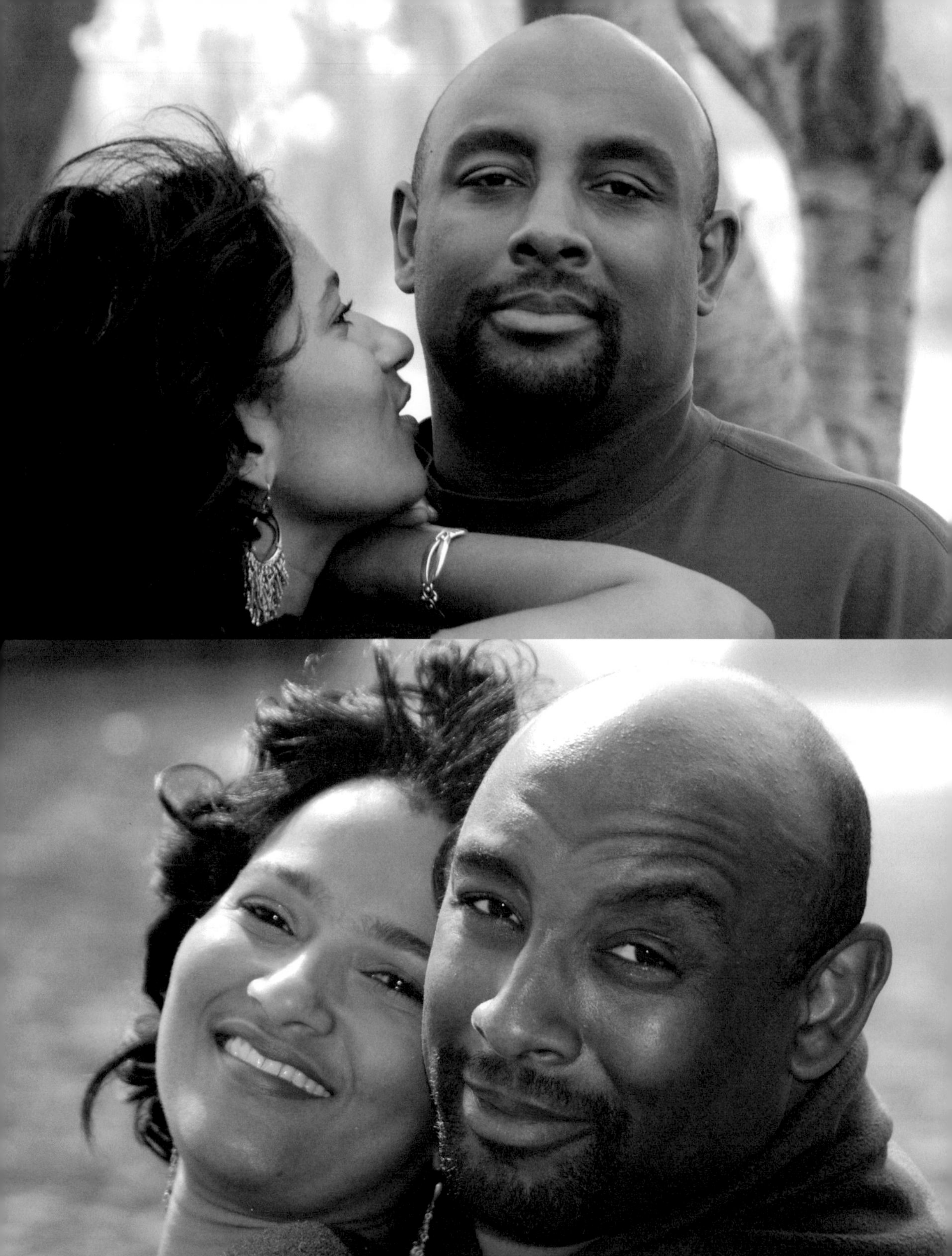

The World Is Not a Pleasant Place to Be

the world is not a pleasant place
to be without
someone to hold and be held by

a river would stop
its flow if only
a stream were there
to receive it

an ocean would never laugh
if clouds weren't there
to kiss her tears

the world is not
a pleasant place to be without
someone

~ *Nikki Giovanni*

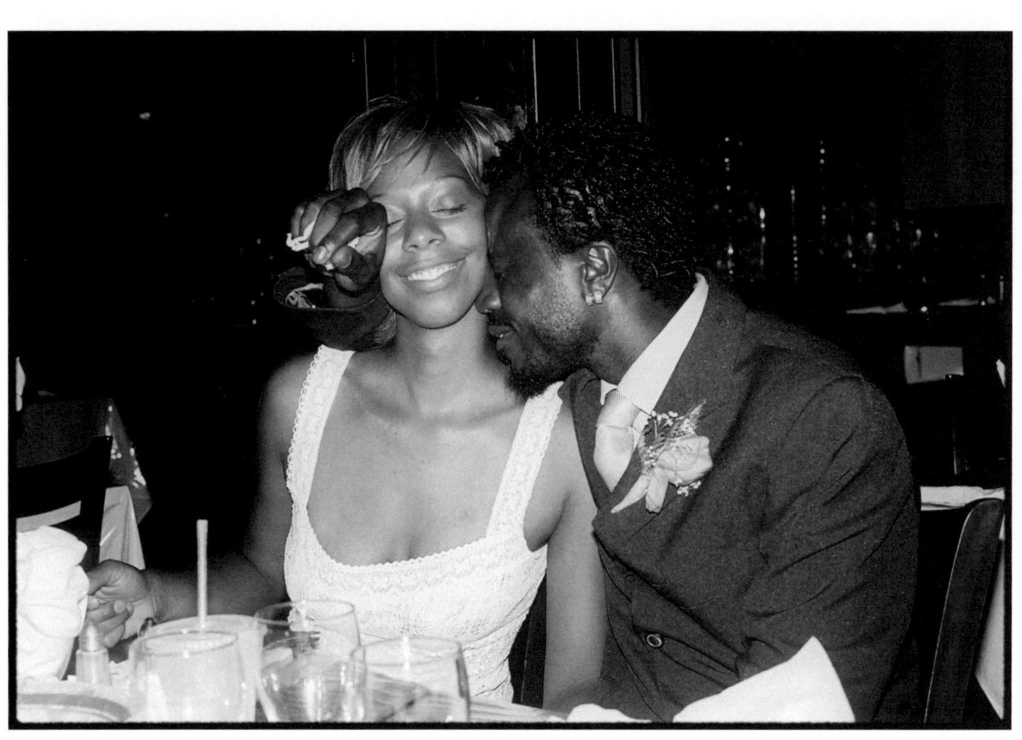

If We Were Quarks

Like all couples, we have our ups
and downs, but the fundamental attraction
remains constant. Inseparable,
we love each other's shadow, people
call us reclusive. Who needs them.
We'd dance to songs so old
there's only a needle in a naked groove,
like random clicks from a Geiger counter.
Every dinner is candle lit and we're never
embarrassed to hold hands in public.
We watch the home movies of our first meeting,
that white hot explosion of emotion,
followed by the countless nights I drifted
through space unaware of the passage of time,
secure in your embrace. When we finally settled,
the mat outside the front door read
Happily Ever After. For who better than us
would know desire cannot be destroyed?

~ Jennifer Gresham

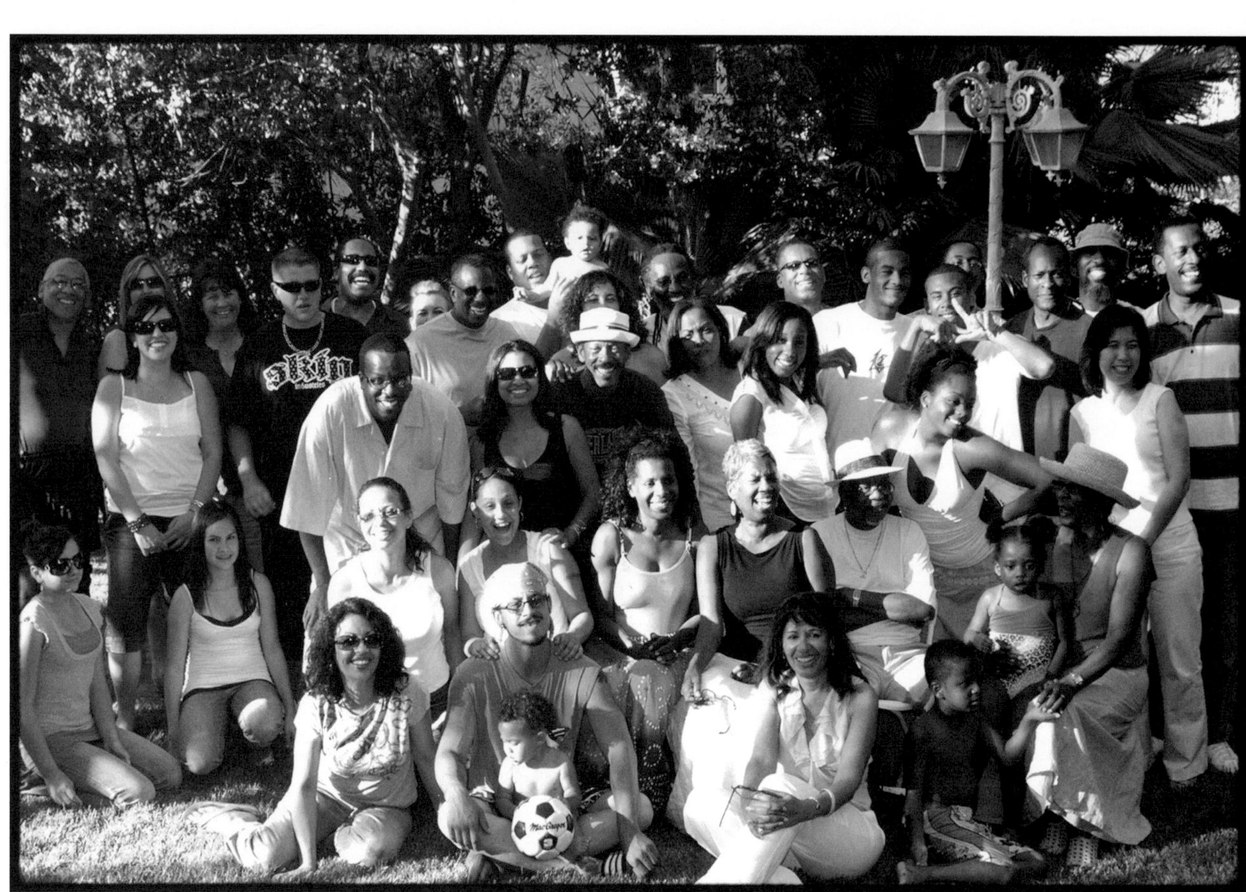

Good Times

My daddy has paid the rent
and the insurance man is gone
and the lights is back on
and my uncle brud has hit
for one dollar straight
and they is good times

Good times
Good times

My mama has made bread
and grampaw has come
and everybody is drunk
and dancing in the kitchen
and singing in the kitchen
of these is good times

Good times
Good times

Oh children think about the
Good times

~ *Lucille Clifton*

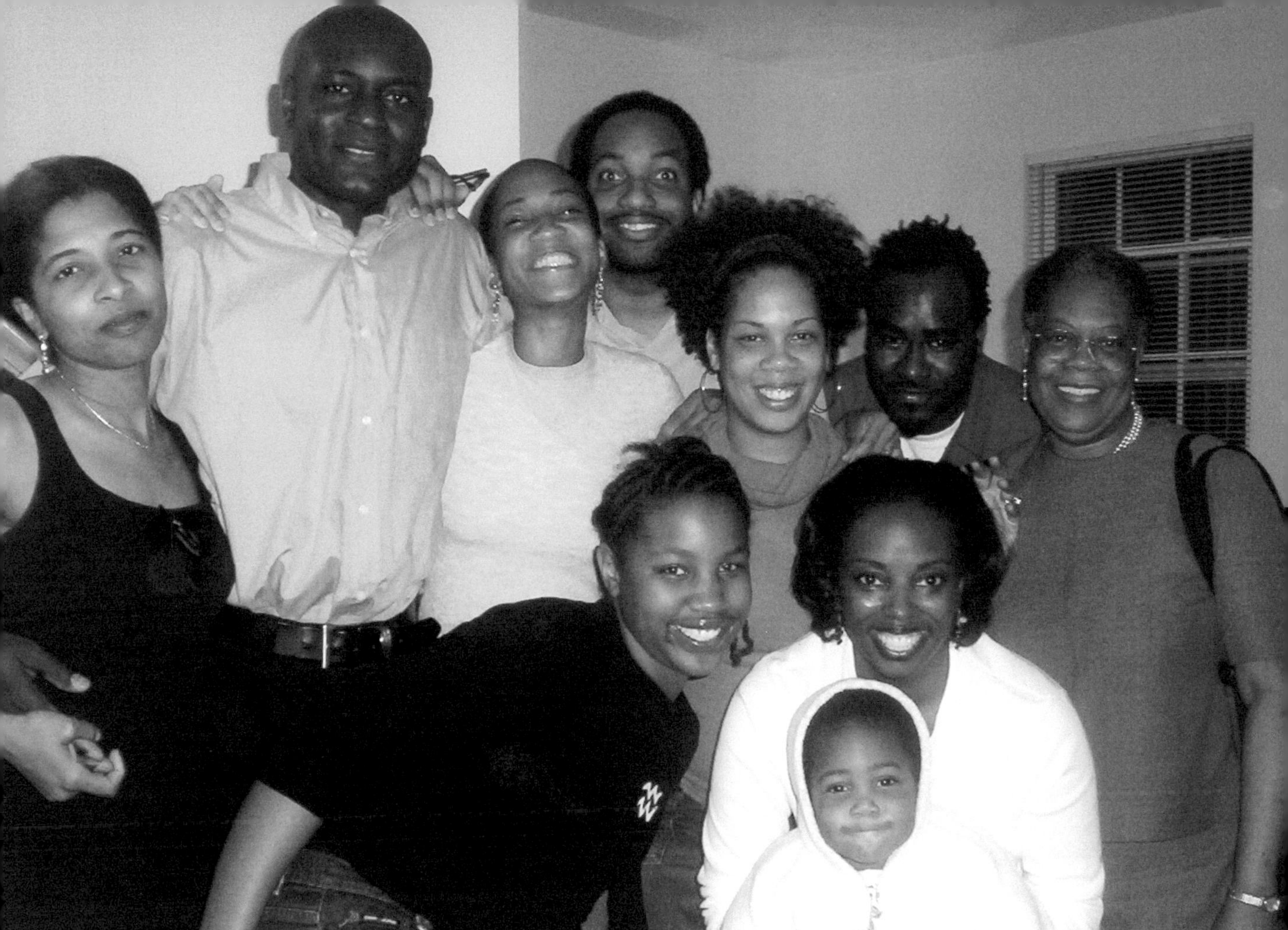

The editor with members of his family at the annual family New Year's Day Karamu

About the Editor

Kwame Alexander, the author of nine books including *Crush: Love Poems* and *Dancing Naked on the Floor,* has written for the stage, television, corporate America, and the federal government. However, what he loves to do most is write poetry about his amazing wife and his phenomenal daughter. He resides in the Washington, DC area, where he serves as producer of the annual *Capital BookFest,* presented by The Washington Post. The Kwame Alexander Papers, a collection of his writings, correspondence, and other professional and personal documents is held at the George Washington University Gelman Library.

About the Contributors

Opal Palmer Adisa is a literary critic, poet, prose writer, storyteller and artist. Her many poetry books and CDs include *Until Judgment Comes*, 2007, *Eros Muse*, 2006, *Caribbean Passion*, 2004, *The Tongue Is a Drum* (poetry/jazz CD with Devorah Major) 2002, *Leaf-of-Life*, 2000, and *Tamarind and Mango Women*, 1992, which won the PEN Oakland/ Josephine Miles Award.

Askhari is an assistant professor of Black Studies; and the moderator of de Griot Space, an online writing workshop for Black writers.

Chrissy Banks lives in Taunton, UK and works as a counsellor. Her poems have been published in magazines and anthologies. Her two books of poetry are *Watching the Home Movies* and *Days of Fire and Flood* (Original Plus 2005).

Roberta Beary's book of poems, *The Unworn Necklace* (Snapshot Press UK, 2007) won first prize in the 2006 Snapshot Press Award Competition. Roberta has worked as an attorney for the past 30 years in New York, Tokyo, and Washington. During the five years Roberta lived in Japan, she discovered the calming spirit of haiku. She is a longtime member of Towpath Poets of the Chesapeake Watershed.

Alicia Benjamin Samuels' poetry has appeared in *Check the Rhyme: An Anthology of Female Poets & Emcees*, *Low Explosions: Writings on the Body*, *Black Arts Quarterly*, *WarpLand*, and SeeingBlack.com, among other venues. She writes frequently for her blog, *Cappuccino Soul*. She lives in Nashville, Tennessee with her husband and daughter.

Sylvia Dianne Beverly. Also known as Ladi Di, "Love Poet," Dianne is a native of Washington, D.C. She has presented poetry around the Washington Metropolitan area, in other states and at the Lewisham Theater in Brixton, London, England. Ms. Beverly is a member of "*Poets in Progress*," under the direction of Poet Laureate of the District of Columbia, Dolores Kendrick. She is the founder/director of "*Girls and Boys with Hearts*," Youth Poetry Group and is a founding member of "*Collective Voices*", sisterhood of poets.

Joelle Biele is the author of *White Summer*, winner of *The Crab Orchard Review* First Book Award and published by Southern Illinois University Press. A former Fulbright scholar, her poems have appeared in *Antioch Review*, *Crazyhorse*, *Gulf Coast*, and *Iowa Review*. She has taught American literature and creative writing at the University of Maryland and Goucher College.

Mawiyah Kai El-Jamah Bomani is a poet whose works has appeared in *The Crab Orchard Review*, *Beyond The Frontier*, *Catch The Fire*, *FreeForm Magazine*, and *Kente Cloth*. Mawiyah currently lives in Shreveport Louisiana with her husband (Nadir Bomani), children (Nzingha, Kambui, Camara and Naima), and mother (Patricia Dean).

Nadir Lasana Bomani is a husband/father/ educator/poet from New Orleans. His work has been published in *Kente Cloth*, *Catch The Fire!!!*, *Dark Eros*, *360° A Revolution Of Black Poets*, *Drumvoices Revue*, and *Beyond The Frontier*. He currently lives in Shreveport with his wonderful wife Mawiyah, and his beautiful babies: Nzingha, Kambui, Camara and Naima.

Ann Reisfeld Boutte was a Juried Poet in the Houston Poetry Fest in 2001 and 2005. Her work has appeared in New Texas, several Texas Poetry Calendars, several June Cotner anthologies and many other publications. She has an M.A. in Journalism from The American University and has been a feature writer for a national wire service.

Kyndall Brown is 11 years old and attends Anne Beers Elementary School in Washington DC. She is a member of the poetry group, Girls and Boys with Hearts. Kyndall also participates in DC Scores at Anne Beers, a program that provides creative writing and soccer activities each day after school. Kyndall also enjoys music, art, and other sports.

Monique Brown is 9 years old. She attends Anne Beers Elementary School in Washington DC. Monique is a member of the poetry group Girls and Boys with Hearts (GBWH).

Leah Browning is the author of two nonfiction books for teens and pre-teens. Her fiction, poetry, essays, and articles have appeared in a variety of publications including *The Saint Ann's Review, Literary Mama, Blood Orange Review, Salome Magazine, Autumn Sky Poetry,* and four anthologies.

Carol Carpenter. "My poems and stories have appeared in online and print publications, including: Margie, Yankee, America, The Pedestal Magazine, Barnwood, Indiana Review, and various anthologies, the most recent is *Not What I Expected* (Paycock Press, 2007). I received the Richard Eberhart Prize for Poetry, and the Jean Siegel Pearson Poetry Award. Formerly a college writing instructor, journalist and trainer, I now write full time in Livonia, MI.

Noni Carter is a 16 year old outstanding student who enjoys writing, music, and helping others. She has two younger sisters who are talented pianists as herself, and an older brother. As a resident of Fairburn, GA, Noni aspires to continue on the path that God has for her. Her first novel, *Good Fortune,* is soon to be published.

Grace Cavalieri is the author of several books, and 21 produced plays. She's produced "The Poet and the Poem" from the Library of Congress on public radio, now in its 30th year. Among honors, Grace holds the Allen Ginsberg Award for Poetry, A Paterson Prize for Poetry, the Pen- Syndicated Fiction Award, the Bordighera Poetry Award, the Folger's inaugural "Columbia Award," and CPB's Silver Medal. Her book *What I Would do For Love* (Poems in the Voice of Mary Wollstonecraft, 1759-1797) is the basis for her new play, "Hyena in Petticoats." Among production awards, her play "Quilting the Sun" received a key to the city of Greenville, S.C. in 2007.

Ching-In Chen is the daughter of Chinese immigrants and a Kundiman Asian American Poet Fellow. A community organizer, she helped to plan the 3rd national Asian Pacific American Spoken Word and Poetry Summit in Boston. Ching-In is currently working on a poetry collection about the travails, heartbreak and adventures of a Chinese-American girl called Xiaomei. She will be entering the MFA program at University of California Riverside this fall.

Lucille Clifton is an award-winning, internationally-acclaimed poet, author, and educator. She won the 2000 National Book Award for Poetry for her book *Blessing the Boats:*

New and Selected Poems (BOA Editions, 2000). She has written 10 collections of poetry and 19 children's books, including the Everett Anderson series.

Maritza Rivera Cohen has been writing poetry in both English and Spanish for nearly 40 years. She is the author of *About You*, has been published in literary magazines, anthologies and online publications, and has been sharing her work in poetry venues in the DC, MD, and VA area for the past ten years.

Christine Compo-Martin Teacher, mother, writer and feminist, Christine Compo-Martin was born and raised in the "North Country" of New York State, an area celebrated for its rich natural beauty and notorious for its brutal winter weather and economic stagnation. Although she intended to write for a profession, the past 19 years have found her teaching middle and high school English at her alma mater in the hamlet of Brasher Falls. Her two children, Emma and Jon, serve as a daily inspiration.

Christopher Conlon's work has appeared widely in magazines and journals including *Poets & Writers, America, Filmfax, Poet Lore, The Long Story,* and *Tennessee Williams Annual Review,* as well as in such anthologies as *Masques V* and *September 11, 2001: American Writers Respond.* Perhaps his best-known book is the original fiction anthology *Poe's Lighthouse* (Cemetery Dance, 2006), in which 23 contemporary writers each complete a little-known story fragment by Edgar Allan Poe. Booklist called the volume a "unique collection" and "must reading for Poe enthusiasts."

Sarah Conover is the author and co-author of books addressing world wisdom traditions for families. Her books include *Kindness: A Treasury of Buddhist Wisdom for Children and Parents; Daughters of the Desert: Remarkable Women from the Christian, Jewish and Muslim Traditions; Ayat Jamilah: Beautiful Signs– A Treasury of Islamic Wisdom for Children and Parents;* and *At Work in Life's Garden: Writers on the Spiritual Adventure of Parenting. Ayat Jamilah* won the 2004 Aesop Award and was cited by Newsweek as one of the best multi-cultural books of 2004.

Matilda W. Cox is currently Director of Advising for the College of Arts & Letters at Old Dominion University where she received her M.A. in English. She is currently pursuing her MFA in Creative Writing. Her poetry has been published in *The Ringing Ear: Black Poets Lean South, Turnings: An Anthology of Women's Writing, Dominion Review* and other literary magazines.

Barbara Crooker's book, *Radiance,* won the 2005 Word Press First Book Award, and was a finalist for the 2006 Paterson Poetry Prize. *Line Dance* is forthcoming from Word in early 2008. Her poems appear in literary journals and anthologies, including *Good Poems for Hard Times* (Garrison Keillor, editor). She has won a number of awards, including the Thomas Merton Poetry of the Sacred Prize.

Alan Davis has published two prize-winning books of his own work and is Senior Editor of New Rivers Press. He teaches in the MFA programs at Stonecoast, a low-residency program associated with the University of Southern Maine, and Minnesota State University Moorhead.

Jeannette Drake is a licensed clinical social worker and author of *Journey Within: A Healing Playbook.* She is a recipient of the Hurston/Wright Foundation Fellowship and is currently working on a novel.

Paul Laurence Dunbar, born in Dayton, Ohio, on June 27, 1872, was the first African-American poet and novelist to attain international recognition. Dunbar was known for his use of dialect, but was also an accomplished poet and novelist in standard English. At age seventeen he published his own newspaper, the Dayton Tattler, an African-American newspaper printed by his high school classmate and friend, Orville Wright. His first book of poems, Oak and Ivy, was published in 1893. The book contained Dunbar's first dialect poem, "A Banjo Song." Dunbar published numerous books of poetry, novels and music during his career. He died in Dayton on February 9, 1906.

Natasha Ria El-Scari is a poetry workshop facilitator and editor of local self-published artists. Her love of the youth is evident in her current position as Project Director of Upward Bound at the University of Missouri-Kansas City. "Most people lie to themselves…I reveal myself."

Gretchen Fletcher can't decide whether she is a teacher who writes or a writer who teaches. She leads writing workshops for Florida Center for the Book and teaches in a private school in Ft. Lauderdale. Her poetry has won awards and been published in San Francisco, Chicago, Houston, Palm Beach, Kansas City, Denver, and Canada.

Adele C. Geraghty is a presentational poet and lecturer, born in Brooklyn, New York and currently residing in the United Kingdom. Her work appears in numerous anthologies, magazines and websites and she is the cofounder of Between These Shores website, pairing poetry with Archaeology. Author of the poetry collection *Skywriting In The Minor Key: Women, Words, Wings,* she is also a recipient of the US National Women's History Award for Excellence in Women's Related Poetry and Essay.

Nikki Giovanni, born June 7, 1943 in Knoxville, Tennessee, is a Grammy-nominated American poet, activist and author. Giovanni is currently a Distinguished Professor of English at the Virginia Polytechnic Institute and State University. She is the author of more than two dozen books, including most recently, *Acolytes: Poems* and *On My Journey Now: Looking at African-American History Through the Spirituals*

Judy Lee Green is an award-winning writer and speaker whose spirit and roots reach deep into the Appalachian Mountains. Tennessee-bred and cornbread-fed, she developed a passion for the written word as a child when inspired to carry a notebook by Daily Planet girl reporter Lois Lane. Published and recognized many times for her work, she is completing a manuscript of creative nonfiction.

Jennifer Gresham received her Ph.D. in biochemistry from the University of Maryland. Her poetry has appeared in over a dozen poetry journals, including *The Atlanta Review, Poet Lore, Beltway Journal, New York Quarterly,* and *The Ledge. Diary of a Cell,* her full-length collection of poems, won the 2004 Steel Toe Books Poetry Prize, judged by Charles Harper Webb.

Joy Harold Helsing lives in the Sierra Nevada foothills of Northern California. As a college undergraduate she won two top awards for poetry in the *Atlantic Monthly* student writing contests. Her work has appeared in a variety of journals and she has published three chapbooks and one book, *Confessions of the Hare* (PWJ Publishing).

Karla Huston is the author of five chapbooks of poetry, most recently: *Flight Patterns,* winner of the *Main Street Rag* Chapbook contest (2003), *Virgins on the Rocks* (Parallel Press, 2004) and *Catch and Release* (Marsh River Editions, 2005). Her poems, reviews and interviews have been published in *Cimarron Review, 5 A.M., Margie, North American Review,* and others.

Ijeoma Thomas. "I am a poet, teacher and performance artist. Co-founder and member of the band Positive Knowledge for over twenty-five years, touring throughout the United States, Europe, the Middle East and Africa. I am also the director of Poetry Out Loud, a literacy project for children and Youth. I was born and raised in Washington, D.C. and currently live in Oakland, CA."

Jason Miccolo Johnson is a professional photographer and author of *Soul Sanctuary.*

Sandra Jones has an MFA in Creative Writing & Publishing Arts from the University of Baltimore. More of her poetry can be found in her book *"I Only Meant To Wet My Feet"* published in October, 2006.

Carolyn Joyner resides in Washington,DC. Her poetry appears in several anthologies including *Mass Ave Review, 360°: A Revolution of Black Poets, Beyond the Frontier,* and *Gathering Ground.* She is a Cave Canem Fellow, and was awarded fellowship grants from the DC Commission for the Arts, and the Virginia Center for the Creative Arts.

Jacqueline Jules. "I am an elementary school librarian and the author of eight children's books. My poetry has appeared in over sixty publications including *The Mid-America Poetry Review, Christian Science Monitor, Calyx, America, Sunstone, Potomac Review,* and *Lullwater Review.* I was a 1999 and 2007 winner in the Arlington Arts Moving Words Poetry Contest and a 2002 recipient of the SCBWI Honor Plaque for Poetry."

Melissa Morelli Lacroix's work has appeared in *TG Magazine, Opus, The Branch Line, In the Red,* and *Express News,* and it has been produced on CBC radio and on stage at the University of Alberta. She lives with her husband and son in Edmonton, Canada.

Pamela Lewis has been widely published and broadcast. She has had two collections and has been translated into French, Greek, Spanish and Chinese. She has given readings in the UK, USA and Greece.

Diane Lockward's collection, *What Feeds Us* (Wind Publications, 2006), was awarded the Quentin R. Howard Prize for Poetry. Her recent work has appeared in *Poet Lore, Spoon River Poetry Review,* and *Prairie Schooner.* Diane works as a poet-in-the schools for the New Jersey State Council on the Arts and the Geraldine R. Dodge Foundation.

Dan Logan. "My poems have been published in litmags, anthologies, and a chamber opera. I have read at numerous venues, including the Hirshhorn Museum, the Yockadot Festival, the D.C. Slam, and the 40th Anniversary March on Washington. I am a foundation executive as well as Chair of the Programming Committee at WPFW Radio."

Frederick Lord is the Assistant Dean of Liberal Arts at Southern New Hampshire University. A collection of his poetry, *What I Made Instead of a Life,* was published in 1996. Lord also teaches English and serves as a poetry editor for *Amoskeag,* SNHU's literary magazine. He and his wife Heather, a painter, live in Hooksett, N. H.

Christina Lovin is the author of *What We Burned for Warmth* (Finishing Line Press). Her work has been widely published and anthologized. An award-winning poet, Lovin is the recipient of many grants (including the 2007 Al Smith Fellowship), from Kentucky Arts Council and Kentucky Foundation for Women. Lovin holds writing workshops and teaches college level writing in Central Kentucky.

Sandra Cohen Margulius's poem, *Women and Birds,* was selected the 2005 winner in the *RUNES, a Review of Poetry, Literary Journal Signals* edition. Her work has also appeared in *The Cream City Review, Radiance Magazine, Hodge Podge Poetry, Women Writing, Buffalo Bones, Robin's Next, A Wise Women's Garden, Hey Listen, Laughing Boy,* and *Sparkle, Sizzle, Hiss.* She completed her MA in Creative Writing in December 2001 at the University of Wisconsin-Milwaukee, inspired by poets/teachers, Susan Firer and William Harrold. Margulius is the mother of three grown children and new grandmother of Eli and Jonah, and continues to live and write in Bayside, Wisconsin with her husband, Simon.

Stephen Mead is an artist and writer living in northeastern NY. His work has been presented extensively online and in print.

Tony Medina is the author of twelve books for adults and children, including *DeShawn Days, Love to Langston, Committed to Breathing* and *Follow-up Letters to Santa From Kids Who Never Got a Response.* Medina's poetry, fiction and essays appear in over thirty anthologies and two CD compilations. Currently, he is an Assistant Professor of Creative Writing at Howard University in Washington, DC.

JJ Michael a graduate of Howard University and University of Maryland, is the author of several publications. Her novels are *Life is Never as It Seems* published by Genesis Press in 2005, and the sequel, *It's Not Over Yet.* Ms. Michael resided in DC, and is currently working on the final novel in the trilogy.

E. Ethelbert Miller is a literary activist. He is the board chairperson of the Institute for Policy Studies (IPS). He is a board member of The Writer's Center and editor of Poet Lore magazine. Since 1974, he has been the director of the African American Resource Center at Howard University. He is an award-winning poet, and has published numerous poetry collections, including *How We Sleep On The Nights We Don't Make Love* (2004), *Whispers, Secrets, and Promises* (Black Classic Press,1998) and the memoir *Fathering Words: The Making of An African American Writer* (2000). Mr. Miller lives in the District of Columbia.

Deanna Nikaido spent her undergraduate years in the Maryland/DC area while attending the University of Maryland then went on to graduate from Art Center College of Design with a BFA in Illustration. She has been featured at venues including the Capital BookFest, and Rumi Festival: Visionary Art Museum. "Vibrating with Silence" is her first poetry book.

Shin Yu Pai is the author of several poetry collections including *Sightings: Selected Works* (1913 Press), *The Love Hotel Poems* (Press Lorentz) and *Equivalence* (La Alameda). She has been awarded writing residencies at Soul Mountain, The MacDowell Colony, The Ragdale Foundation, and Taipei Artist Village.

Michelle J. Pinkard is a poet, writer, and educator who lives in Phoenix, AZ. Her collection of poetry *The Eye of the Tornado: Fifty Poems for Rhyme and Reason* was released to rave reviews. Her work has been published in numerous anthologies and collections. Pinkard is currently pursuing a PhD in literature at Arizona State University.

Andrea Potos' full-length collection of poems entitled *Yaya's Cloth* was recently published by Iris Press. Her poems appear widely in journals and anthologies, including *Women's Review of Books, Poetry East, Prairie Schooner, Mothers & Daughters* (Random House), *Claiming the Spirit Within* (Beacon Press) and many others. She lives in Madison, Wisconsin.

William Reichard is an author and educator. His most recent collection, "This Brightness," was published by Mid-List Press in April 2007.

Regena Reigns is a model, actress, and spoken word artists who resides in the Washington, DC area.

Susan Rich is author of *The Cartographer's Tongue: Poems of the World,* which won the PEN USA and Peace Corps Writers Awards. White Pine Press recently published her second collection of poems, *Cures Include Travel.* She lives in Seattle, WA but has worked in Bosnia, Gaza, Southern Africa, and West Africa. Recent poems appear in *Bellevue Literary Review, North American Review,* and *Witness.*

Jason Kelly Richards was born in Kentucky in a classic year for Chevrolets, raised in North Carolina during the best decade of music and currently resides in the Sunshine State. His work has appeared in several print publications including The Chiron Review and *Pearl,* plus online at *PoetsCanvas, Underground Voices, Red Booth Review, AntiMuse* and many others.

Katy Richey has been published in *Beltway Poetry Quarterly* and has performed poetry at venues and festivals in the Washington D.C. area including the *2006 Capital Book Festival.* She teaches English in Silver Spring, Maryland.

Charles P. Ries lives in Milwaukee, Wisconsin. His narrative poems, short stories, interviews and poetry reviews have appeared in over one hundred and seventy print and electronic publications. He has received four Pushcart Prize nominations for his writing. He is the author of *The Fathers We Find,* a novel, and five books of poetry–the most recent entitled, *The Last Time.* He is a member of the Wisconsin Poet Laureate Commission.

Kim Roberts is the author of two books of poems: *The Kimnama* (Vrzhu Press, 2007), and *The Wishbone Galaxy* (WWPH, 1984). She is the editor of *Beltway Poetry Quarterly,* an on-line journal, and has been the recipient of grants from the National Endowment for the Humanities, the DC Commission on the Arts, the Humanities Council of Washington, DC, and has been a writer-in-residence at eleven artist colonies.

C. Alison Rollins was born and raised in St. Louis, Missouri. She is a psychology major attending Howard University in Washington, D.C. She has performed for Mari Evans and Nikki Giovanni at a annual Heart's Day Tribute done by Howard University. She is 19 years old and an aspiring poet.

Matthue Roth is a performance poet and young-adult novelist. He has filmed for *Def Poetry Jam, Rock the Vote,* and toured nationally. His first novel, *Never Mind the Goldbergs,* was published by Scholastic. He lives with his wife on the road, and he keeps a secret online diary at www.matthue.com.

Metta Sama (previously Lydia Melvin) has published one book of poems, *South of Here* (New Issues Press, 2005) and has had poems published or forthcoming in *The Crab Orchard Review, Diner, Cream City Review, Shade, The Baltimore Review, hubbub, Kestrel,* among others. She lives in upstate New York, where she and her lover are both PhD students at SUNY-Binghamton.

Carly Sachs teaches creative writing at George Washington University. Her first book of poems, the steam sequence, won the Washington Writers' Publishing House book prize in 2006. With Reb Livingston, she curates Lolita and Gilda's Burlesque Poetry Hour at Bar Rouge.

Darlene Anita Scott Delaware native, holds a B.A. from Spelman College and an M.F.A. in Creative Writing from Virginia Commonwealth University. darlene's poetry appears in anthologies including *Homegirls Make Some Noise, Growing Up Girl,* and *Role Call,* and has also been featured in international publications including *Love Poems for the Media Age* and *X* literary magazine. She has received grants from the Virginia Commission for the Arts and has been a fellow at the Virginia Center for the Creative Arts, the Hurston Wright Foundation, and the Julia and David White Artists' Colony in Ciudad Colon, Costa Rica.

Derek Sheffield won *North American Review's* James Hearst Poetry Prize judged by Li-Young Lee. He has published one chapbook of poems, *A Mouthpiece of Thumbs* (Blue Begonia 2000), and his work has appeared in *The Georgia Review, Ecotone, Orion, Poet Lore, Margie/The American Journal of Poetry,* the *Anthology of Magazine Verse & Yearbook of American Poetry,* and several anthologies.

Glen Sorestad is a Saskatoon poet who has had over 15 volumes of his poetry published, has appeared in nearly 50 anthologies and texts, and has been translated into a half-dozen languages.

Judith Strasser is the author of a memoir, *Black Eye: Escaping a Marriage, Writing a Life,* and two poetry collections, *The Reason/Unreason Project,* winner of the Lewis-Clark Expedition Award, and *Sand Island Succession.* She co-edited the new anthology, *On Retirement: 75 Poems,* and her poetry has appeared in many literary journals and anthologies.

Kathleen Sullivan. "I am a newly minted MFA graduate with a smattering of published poems. I live in Maine, have two grown."

Lynn Tait is a poet from Sarnia, Ontario Canada. Her work has appeared in *Windsor Review, Contemporary Verse 2, Re:al, Timber Creek Review, touchstone,* and various Canadian and American anthologies. She has also published a chapbook *Breaking Away.*

Angela Boykin Turnbull is a poet and editor who performed her work throughout the U.S., London, England and most recently at the Muse'e du Louvre in Paris, France. She helped edit the Capital Book Festival's first publication, *The Way I Walk* and her work has been published in *360°: A Revolution of Black Poets*. Angela was the former president of the African American Writer's Guild and a recent participant in the Jenny McKean Moore Writer's Program at George Washington University.

Davi Walders' poetry and prose has appeared in more than 200 anthologies and journals, including *The American Scholar, JAMA, Lilith, Lonely Planet,* and *Travelers Tales*. She developed and directs the Vital Signs Writing Project at NIH in Bethesda, MD which was funded by The Witter Bynner Foundation for Poetry. Gifts, her third collection of poetry, was commissioned by the Milton Murray Foundation for Philanthropy. Her work has been choreographed and performed in NYC and read by Garrison Keillor on Writer's Almanac.

Phylis Warady. With three children under five, Phylis Warady began writing to save her sanity. Her award-winning light verse and short fiction recently appeared in *Dan River Anthology, 4th Annual Northwoods Anthology, Not What I Expected* (The Unpredictable Road from Womanhood to Motherhood) and *Oasis Journal*.

Christine West lives in a pottery village in the very centre of France. She writes full-time now and lets her husband do the potting. Her poems have been published in several poetry reviews. She worked hard at school, trained at art college, worked for an airline and brought up four children (her own son and three steps). Now her time is her own and life is good. Poetry is her favourite thing.

Sandra L. West's work has been published in *Essence, Emerge, Chickenbones,* and *Goucher Quarterly*. She is a member of The Harlem Writers Guild.

Mary Sherman Willis is a writer living in Virginia and teaching at George Washington University. Her poems and reviews have appeared in *The New Republic, Poet Lore, The Iowa Review, Shenandoah, The Hudson Review,* and online at *Archipelago.org*.

Shana Yarborough is a Spelman College graduate and a MFA graduate of the University of Baltimore. She is the author of a book of poetry entitled *Looking For Love In All The Small Spaces*. She lives in Baltimore, Maryland.

About the Photographers

Rodney Bailey of Wedding Photojournalism by Rodney Bailey (www.RodneyBailey.com) is a photojournalist in the purest sense. He has documented weddings for sixteen years in this unobtrusive (and now, trendy) approach and is one of the most sought after wedding photographers in Washington DC. Rodney's work has been featured in many of today's top bridal magazines including *Modern Bride, The Knot, 'I Do' for Brides, Grace Ormonde Wedding Style, Engaged, Elegant Bride* and *Wedding Dresses*. Rodney is also commissioned for corporate, fashion and commercial photography projects, though weddings still remain his passion. He has captured images for the Library of Congress, *Vogue* and Disney, as well as Oprah Winfrey and *O Magazine*. Rodney has been voted the "Top Photojournalist" in the *Washingtonian Magazine* for ten consecutive years and is featured in *Grace Ormonde Wedding Style Magazine* as one of the top five photographers in Washington DC. During his down time, Rodney can still be found behind the camera; however his subjects are sharks and sea life as he is an avid scuba diver and underwater photographer.

Bonita F. Bing, a native Washingtonian, has been photographing for the past 25 years. In 2002, she was elected as the first woman president of The Exposure Group African American Photographers Association, Inc. In 2003, she received the Community Service Award from The Exposure Group. Bonita received a BA Degree in Speech Communications from the University of Pittsburgh in Pittsburgh, Pennsylvania, and currently serves as a Network Operations Specialist for the U.S. Senate.

Michael DiBari has been a working photojournalist for the past 15 years. His work has been published in a variety of newspapers and magazines including *The Washington Post, The Los Angeles Times, The Baltimore Sun, The Detroit Free Press* and *Time* magazine. He is based out of Columbia, Maryland and lives there with his wife and two sons.

Martha FitzSimon trained at the International Center of Photography in New York City. Martha has worked with some of the best photographers in the country. Her award-winning work has been shown at galleries in New York and Washington DC. Before becoming a professional photographer, Martha was a journalist and writer in New York. She has a master's degree in journalism from the University of Texas at Austin.

Nataki Hewling is a photographer, children's talent agent, and Assistant Photo Editor for *Time for Kids* magazine. With her HOLGA camera, she captures honesty and raw emotion. She has worked on several educational books and classroom magazines as a Photo Editor, including the Read 180 series produced by Scholastic, Inc. Her photo collection of mothers and children was used in a publication of "The Intelligence Group."

Jason Miccolo Johnson is an award-winning documentary, editorial, and fine art photographer. A native Memphian and Howard University alumnus, he is perhaps best recognized for his trademark shooting style that focuses on the subject's eyes and hands. He is the author of *Soul Sanctuary: Images of the African American Worship Experience* and the recipient of the *ArtMaker* award from the HistoryMakers organization.

Shevry Lassiter, the owner of Sure Shot Photography, enjoys capturing images depicting city and family life as well as history making events. Shevry is a member of the Photography Ministry at Greater Mt. Calvary Holy Church in Washington, DC, and a member of the Exposure Group, a national group of African American photography professionals. Shevry's passion for event photography led her to a position as one of the Official Photographers for Tom Joyner's Fantastic Voyage in 2007. Shevry is a native Washingtonian, a member of the Professional Photographer's Association, a wife, a mother, and a grandmother.

Reneé Michele's photojournalistic style and abillity to create unique portraiture are drawn from her experience in wedding, portrait, fashion, and commercial photography. Shooting for over twelve years, her goal is to create images that capture the personality of her subjects. She was voted *The Knot 2007 Best of Weddings Pick* and one of the area's Best Photographers by *Washingtonian Magazine*, 2006-2007.

Carol Siegel, BA, American University, MA, Lesley College, has taught Photography to all age groups and currently leads Expressive Art groups in Adult Day Care Centers for Arts For the Aging in Bethesda, Maryland. Her photographs have been published and exhibited widely including The Corcoran Gallery of Art, Washington, D.C. They are in the permanent collection of the Black History Museum in Alexandria, VA.

Frank Solomon has over twenty years experience as a commercial photographer. He is the official photographer of the Capital BookFest presented by *The Washington Post*.

Index of First Lines

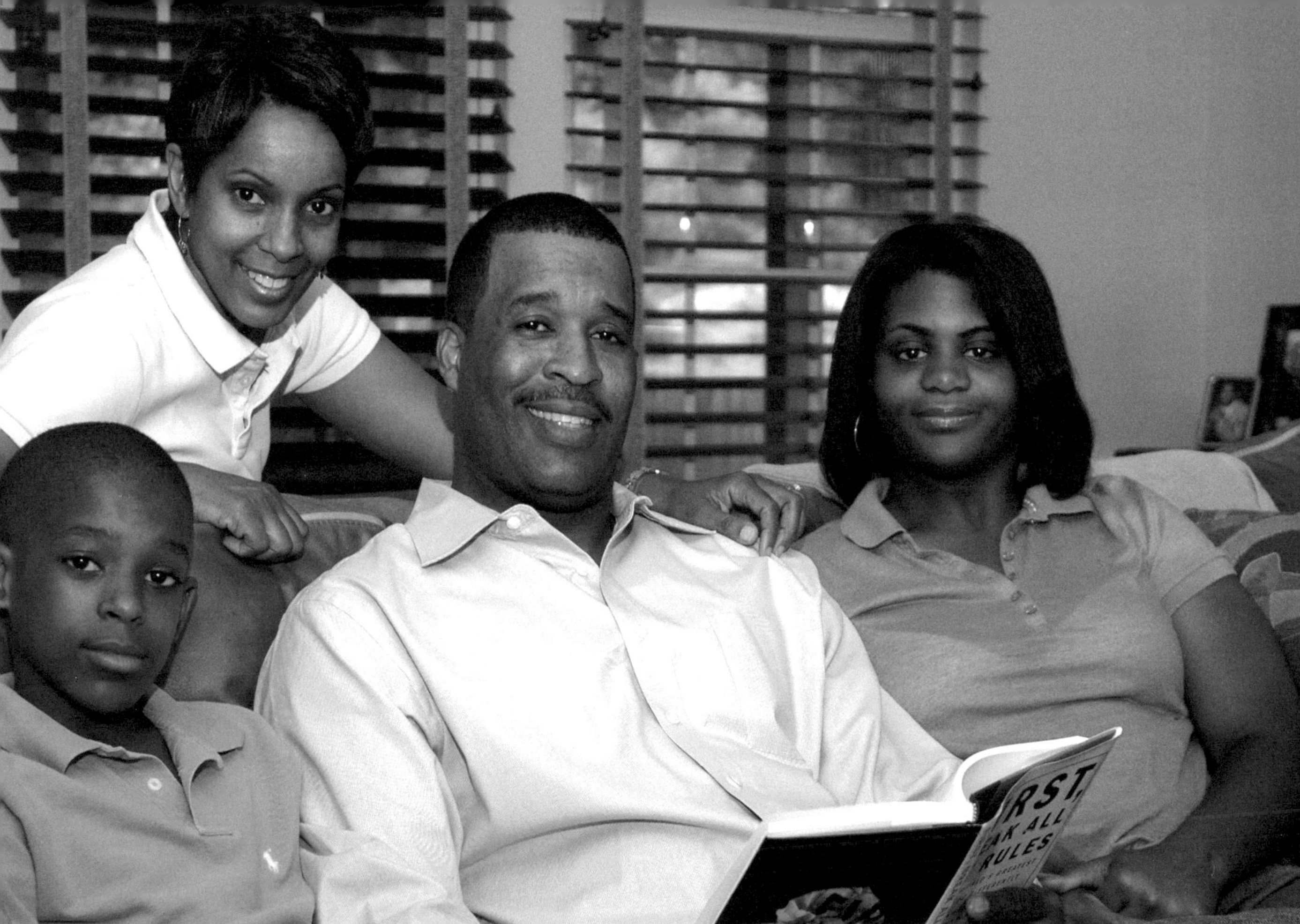

Keith Singletary and family, owners of Chick-fil-A Capital Centre (Largo, MD), underwriters of this project

Acknowledgements

Friends, artists, and mentors who supported me in this endeavor. Capital BookFest 2007 for the opportunity–Gabrielle Faulcon, LaWanda Amaker, Stephanie Stanley, Nandi Alexander, and Frank Solomon. Many thanks to the poets and photographers who brought their art to the front door of my vision. This project would never have come to light without the commitment, professionalism, and genuine cheer of the editorial assistants–Your art is only matched by your beauty and class. My parents, siblings, family, for giving me the time and space to finish this book–during vacation. As Prince George's County's unofficial patron of the literary arts, Keith Singletary and Chick-fil-A Capital Centre made this enormous project possible, and I am forever grateful.

You don't choose

your family.

They are God's gift to you,

as you are to them.

~ DESMOND TUTU